HOW A NICE JEWISH BOY SURVIVED
FIVE YEARS IN AMERICA'S DARKEST PRISONS

PRIVILEGE
LOST

JOSHUA ELYASHIV

MANHATTAN
BOOK GROUP

Published by Manhattan Book Group
447 Broadway 2nd Floor, #354, New York, NY 10013
(212) 634-7677
www.manhattanbookgroup.com

Printed in the United States of America.
ISBN-13: 978-1-962987-04-2

For Bonnie, who sees my ugliest scars and still loves me,
For Leora, who contains the best parts of me,
and for Pat-our families will never know the weight we carry.

I swear they broke my jaw. It was so swollen that I couldn't cry out. I couldn't scream for help. I couldn't beg for my mother. I couldn't even whisper the words, "I'm sorry." I knew that today was going to be the day that I died; this was when they were finally going to kill me.

I tried to curl into a fetal position to protect as much of myself as possible. I wasn't very successful, though, because my hands were cuffed behind my back and my feet were shackled together while four men kicked me with combat boots and steel-toed shoes. Fire lanced from my fingers to my shoulders as one of them stomped on my hands and the handcuffs bit further into my wrists. I tried to swallow the vomit that came up immediately after a boot connected with my kidney, because I knew that if I got puke on any of the men, the beatings would intensify. I tried desperately not to make a sound as the tears streamed down my face. There was an explosion of pain in my head, and everything went dark.

Despite the pounding in my head and the throbbing in my jaw that was ballooned to the size of Texas, I tried to open my eyes; one of them was swollen shut, but the other opened after an eternity of trying. White. All I saw was white. I realized that I was facedown and the white that I was seeing was the corner between the concrete wall and the floor, inches from my face. I slowly, gingerly pushed myself up into a sitting position while the world spun. It took a few seconds to remember where I was. This was the second time that I had been beaten unconscious today, I think. Although I don't remember how I got back here, I was back. Again.

I was in a concrete box, approximately seven-by-ten feet with a stainless steel toilet on one wall and a rusty steel bunk on the other wall. A cloudy six-by-six-inch plexiglass window allowed a small amount of light into the box from the solid steel door. I gently massaged my wrists as I recognized that I was back in the cell. I glanced down at myself and saw that there were fresh bloodstains on the front of my shirt, and I realized that my lip, nose, and swollen-shut eye were bleeding. I thought it was Tuesday, but I wasn't sure. I also thought it was August, but it could have been September. And I guessed that it was late afternoon because I had only been beaten twice so far and the evening crew had not arrived to have their go. My lips were cracked, and I was so thirsty. Unbearably thirsty. They'd had the water to the cell turned off for a week, maybe longer.

As I stood up to go drink from the toilet bowl, I collapsed onto the floor when my knee gave out from the torn ACL. I took a moment to just lie there on the floor. Everything hurt too much to attempt getting up again. My stomach grumbled, and I couldn't remember the last time I'd had something to eat. Was it two weeks ago that I was given a slice of white bread to eat, or three? I wasn't entirely sure.

My name is Joshua, and this is my story.

AWAKENING

"Bork! Attorney visit!" The words reverberated through the air, emanating from a chorus of metallic voices that echoed from multiple loudspeakers.

My heart soared with anticipation. Today was going to be the day, the moment I would receive the long-awaited good news that this was all just a grave error and I would finally return home. I held unwavering faith in the system's ability to correct itself—why wouldn't it? Life always worked out, especially for me. After all, even the wise Martin Luther King Jr. proclaimed that "we shall overcome because the arc of the moral universe is long, but it bends toward justice." Now, it was my turn to taste that justice.

Dressing with a speed reminiscent of my Marine Corps days, I almost felt as if I could bend time itself. I was going home! I knew it in my bones. I had committed no wrongdoing, harmed no one, broken no laws, not even caused offense to anyone. Moreover, I was well spoken, possessed a captivating charm, and was undeniably attractive. I did not hail from a troubled background, nor did I bear the weight of a criminal record. My presence here had to be a terrible mistake, and everyone knew it.

It was merely a matter of going through the motions to rectify this error, and I had no doubt it would be resolved.

While waiting by the entrance, my mind raced with exhilaration. What would be my first meal upon release? Or perhaps I craved a refreshing shower and clean clothes to wash away the past. Oh, the bliss of clean clothing and the warm embrace of my beloved dog, Abby!

With a resounding buzz, the door swung open. After what felt like an eternity confined in a small concrete vestibule, a guard arrived to escort me to meet Yvonne, my attorney. An intoxicating blend of excitement and positivity overwhelmed me, nearly causing me to skip like a schoolgirl as I traversed one corridor after another. Furthermore, my previous encounters with Yvonne had been delightful. She possessed a witty sense of humor, an endearing sweetness, and even a hint of flirtation. Our interactions had been so amicable that I intended to invite her for a coffee date once I had cleaned up in a few days.

Finally, I found myself in a small room, handcuffed to the table. Yet an inexplicable tranquility enveloped me. In just a moment, everything would return to normal, relegating the past few months to a mere unpleasant memory, something to laugh about later. "Remember that time when the government and the police made a mistake and came after me? Hilarious! Absolutely ridiculous! I'm just glad it's all cleared up!"

However, the instant Yvonne stepped into the room, a disconcerting sense washed over me. Her demeanor was serious, stern even. No trace of playfulness remained; it was all business now. Before she even uttered a word, an ominous premonition gripped me tightly, heralding an impending doom.

"Mr. Bork," she said coldly, "you must come to terms with the severity of this situation. Going home is not an option for you anytime soon."

"B-but—," I stammered.

"We need to discuss our options," she interjected.

Her voice seemed to drift from a great distance, as if emanating from the far end of a long tunnel. It felt like a dreadful nightmare, and all I had to do was wake up.

I forced a smile. "I was just about to ask you out for coffee. Perhaps next month instead of—"

"Mr. Bork," she interrupted, her tone firm. "This is no laughing matter. I'm sorry, but you need to realize that you are facing years."

"What!"

"I don't know why they've chosen to make an example out of you, but that's exactly what they're doing."

I don't recall saying goodbye or the journey back to my cell. The sound of the door locking didn't register. All I remember is the overwhelming feeling of suffocation within the confines of those gray-and-blue walls, illuminated relentlessly by fluorescent lights.

How had a person like me, a genuinely good individual, ended up in a place like this?

Pinellas County Jail—how did I wind up here? A respectable Jewish young man such as myself?

The suffocating humidity weighed heavily, and the pungent odor of unwashed bodies filled the air, affirming that this had to be a terrible mistake.

This place, it was ceaselessly loud, a constant cacophony. It felt as though every aspect of it was engineered to maximize noise, resembling a perpetually raucous high school cafeteria. Conversations swirled in languages foreign to me, laced with slang I didn't comprehend, the urban culture that remained beyond my comprehension.

What was I doing here?

Steel tables, concrete walls, and ceilings dominated the surroundings, with at least a third of the men incessantly pounding on the tables, aspiring to be the next rap star. The reverberating noise exerted physical pressure on the atmosphere, as if a grown man piggybacked on my shoulders. I tried shoving toilet paper in my ears, pulled a pillow over my face, but nothing could silence the clamor that refused to relent.

I replayed my meeting with Yvonne in my mind, my heart sinking and thoughts racing. Slowly but surely, it dawned on me that slipping away from this nightmarish existence was an implausible fantasy.

How did I end up here? How could something like this happen to an individual like me?

I wasn't a criminal.

I did not smoke, drink, or use drugs.

At twenty-five years old, I hadn't even tried marijuana!

I followed rules diligently, never exceeding the speed limit, never jaywalking, never indulging in revelry. In fact, social gatherings held little allure for me—I was always tucked into bed by 9:00 p.m.

I was the quintessential law-abiding citizen.

Born into a highly educated and prosperous family, with a registered nurse for a mother, three aunts who were also nurses, and an uncle who practiced law. My father, a biomedical engineer and the son of Holocaust survivors, boasted a sister who held a dean's position at Northeastern University, while my uncle Kerry specialized in graduate-level philosophy.

We were an intelligent, stable, and morally upright Jewish family residing in an affluent neighborhood. Our weekends were devoted to synagogue visits and observing kosher traditions. Furthermore, both of my parents were actively involved throughout my upbringing. Our home was devoid of drugs, and alcohol rarely made an appearance.

So, how on earth did I find myself behind these bars?

I attended reputable schools, even skipping a grade from second to fourth. And during summer break, instead of engaging in playful activities or visiting arcades, I remained at home, diligently learning cursive from my mother.

What kind of child willingly chooses to stay home and practice cursive?

My parents never allowed me to buy lunch at school. I never possessed fashionable clothing or popular toys. Wearing hand-me-downs from older cousins, I was the teacher's pet who effortlessly answered every question. I wasn't popular or cool; I was a dedicated scholar and a compassionate soul. I freely provided answers to my classmates during tests so they could keep their grades up and remain involved in extracurricular activities. I worked in the school store, and if someone lacked the means to acquire what they needed, I dipped into my own savings to help them out.

On the edge of the campus, I would seek solace under the shade of a tree, completing my homework, and sharing my lunch with a fellow student who sought refuge there, hiding his lack of lunch money. I suspected he might be on the autism spectrum, but I couldn't be sure. What I did know was that his parents were deceased, and he resided with his grandparents and lived on a limited income. He never brought lunch to school and was perpetually strapped for cash. On the occasions when I was granted permission to use a classroom during lunchtime for some air-conditioned reading, I discreetly brought him along. While he immersed himself in comic books, I happily shared my meal with him.

I defended this individual against bullies, despite not possessing any inherent toughness. I myself was a scrawny, undersized kid.

How did I end up in a state prison?

I wasn't a rebel. In truth, I cherished structure. I was a bookworm, one of those youngsters who felt more at ease conversing with older, wiser individuals. Video games and Pokémon held little allure for me. Raised around Holocaust survivors, I relished listening to the life experiences of those who had accrued wisdom and knowledge beyond my own years.

Perhaps it was this longing for structure that led me to enroll in the Sarasota Military Academy in 2001. I begged my parents to send me there. What kind of child pleads to attend military school? I yearned for purpose, meaning, something more profound than what the average high school could offer. Within two years, I became fencing team captain, led the drill team, and secured membership in the National Honor Society. I even graduated early at the age of sixteen to commence my college journey.

What kind of scumbag begins college at sixteen?

In all honesty, I was a bookworm with a nonexistent social life.

Returning for the graduation ceremony with my peers in 2006, I graduated second in my class, surpassed only by a classmate who had an additional semester in Honors JROTC. Standardized tests never posed a challenge—I consistently achieved top scores, reaching the ninety-ninth percentile on the FCATs and SATs. Additionally, I garnered a congressional nomination from Congresswoman Catherine Harris to the United States Naval Academy in Annapolis, an accomplishment I cherished deeply.

What sort of criminal earns admission to Annapolis?

I'll tell you the answer: none!

I did not belong here, among thieves, scoundrels, addicts, and pedophiles. I was a decent and upright young man, someone who did not deserve to be labeled a criminal. I simply did not belong in this hellish place.

Two weeks after Yvonne's visit, a guard shoved me, and in response, I pushed him back. Like moths to a flame, the guards descended upon me, battering me mercilessly. Pain exploded within my head, and then everything faded into darkness.

THE PRICE OF BISCUITS

It had been two weeks since I signed my plea deal, and I was just waiting for the Bureau of Prisons to come pick me up. Five years of my life would be gone just because I chose to defend myself. Then again, could've been worse; I could've been slapped with thirty years like nothing. Going forward, I decided that I wasn't going to take shit from anybody anymore. After all, what's the worst they could do to me? Send me to jail? Battery on a detainee carried a maximum of five years concurrent with my sentence. As long as I didn't *kill* anybody, they couldn't give me any extra time no matter how badly I behaved.

Sitting on my bunk before breakfast and reading a book, I start-ed thinking about how wonderful it was to be out of confinement, just to be able to read books and have conversations with people. My new bunkmate was a big man named Rod Huggins, six feet five inches and well over three hundred pounds. He went to college on a football scholarship and was a linebacker until he blew out his knee. Rod didn't say a whole lot because he was still fighting his charges, but I knew he was a kingpin, and not just a self-proclaimed one. He was the head of a criminal organization that was under indictment for RICO charges—something to do with opioids and painkiller distribution. Every person beneath him had snitched for a plea deal, but Rod still refused to speak to the police. He also had a major lawsuit going against the police and the correctional officers for cruel and unusual punishment, physical abuse, and violence, being denied medical attention, being starved, and bunch of other civil rights violations that didn't sound too different from what I had been going through. On this, we bonded.

Rod was generally pleasant person, easy to be around, but he was diabetic, and when his blood sugar dropped, he transformed. One morning, he stood up and said to me, "You're going to give me your biscuits and gravy this morning."

Sensing danger, I got off of my bunk and faced him.

"No," I said, "I'm not. I will *sell* you my breakfast, but I'm not giving it to you for free."

Rod may have been massive, but he was also slow. Like a grizzly bear, he swung his enormous left hand in a wild circle toward my head—the thing was nearly as big as my face! Still, the lumbering behemoth that he was, I easily ducked, and Rod screamed as his fist smashed into the steel of the bunk. As Rod turned to swing at me again with his undamaged right hand, I threw the fastest three-strike combo of my life. Right, left, right—all striking him in the fat pouch where his neck should have been. As Rod grabbed his throat gurgling and collapsed toward me, I tried to get out of the way, but Rod landed on me— I landed upside down with this giant gorilla on top of me. My hips and legs were still on my bunk, but my shoulders were on the floor. *Jujitsu 101: Shrimping.* I framed up with my arms and shrimped out from underneath Rod. He slumped further onto the ground as I rolled onto my right side and got out from underneath him. As I got my feet under me, I was already throwing punches at his head—ten fast ones, my fists flew like I was pedaling a bicycle with my hands, each one impacting the sides and back of his skull and neck, then nine more as he was trying to cover his head.

"Josh, look out!" someone in the dorm shouted.

I straightened up and turned clockwise with my right arm already protecting my face, but I didn't turn fast enough and felt the sharp sting of a wooden cane crack against my shoulder blade and upper back. My right arm, the one that was protecting my face, shot out and around, trapping the arm and the cane under my right armpit as my left fist smashed into the face of the young man who'd hit me. He stumbled back. I kept the cane.

"Leave him alone!" he screamed. "You're hurting him!" Then he brushed himself off and said, "I've studied the secret art of Machu Picchu! Don't make me hurt you."

I almost laughed. This young man was a harmless, schizophrenic vagrant, in custody for panhandling and loitering. I tossed the cane on the floor and went to sit next to my workout partner in front of the TV. He was sitting on a stainless steel bench attached to a stainless steel table that was bolted to the concrete floor. The morning news was playing.

I took a deep breath. "Thanks for looking out, man. I appreciate it."

But he just looked over his shoulder in the direction of my bunk and said, "Heads up."

I turned just in time to see Rod Huggins careening toward me in a lumbering lurch. I stood up and pivoted counterclockwise to face what was coming head on. I met his forward momentum by punching him in the face with my left hand, one hard jab. His forward momentum was so great that although I was hitting him, I was also being pushed back. My left leg caught the corner of the bench as Rod tackled me to the ground.

Have you ever had a three-hundred-pound tub of lard sit on you? Twice before breakfast?

Up until this moment, neither had I.

Rod immediately grabbed my left and right wrists, pinning them to the ground on either side of my head, straddling my waist with his knees on the ground. It was bad, but even worse because it didn't seem like he was gonna be able to get up either. I attempted to shrimp out again, but this time I was unsuccessful. Rod let go of my left hand so he could rear back to punch me.

The moment he did, I did a sit up and drove my left elbow into the most accessible target, his ginormous belly. The elbow straight to the belly was enough to interrupt his strike, as he grabbed my left arm and slammed it to the ground again. I kept squirming back, attempting to trap one of his legs and sweep him off me or create enough space to shrimp out. When he let go of my hand again to rear back for a punch, I bucked my hips up and did a crunch to slam my elbow into his stomach again. Again, his punch was interrupted as he collapsed forward, pinning me to the ground.

We repeated this dance about a dozen times, slowly moving from one end of the bench to the other. I managed to get my head just under the edge of the bench—I hoped this would allow me to use Rod's size against him by preventing him from being able to strike or control me—too many obstacles, too much confined space.

As Rod tried to hit me one more time, my arm shot up, and I grabbed the front of his shirt. Then I thrust my hips up as I threw my head and shoulders back to the ground, pulling Rod's face with me, slamming his eye into the corner of the bench—once and then again—*bang bang!* His eye started bleeding just a little bit, and you would think that after having your head slammed into the corner of a steel table twice, you *might* back off. Not a chance. Rod tried to hit me again and again.

I yanked down even harder this time as Rod let go of my other hand in an attempt to brace himself against the table and stop another hit to his eye. This was just the opening I needed—now both of my hands were free. For just a millisecond, I contemplated shrimping again, but I had nowhere to go—I was wedged between a steel bench bolted to the floor and a table bolted to the floor. No way was my six three, 220-pound frame gonna get in there to shrimp and maneuver. Instead, I did a Hail Mary, grabbing his collar with both hands and yanking down as hard as I could while throwing my hips up with all my might.

Finally! It was more than Rod could handle, and his arm slipped, or collapsed. He turned his face, trying to avoid a direct hit, but this only made matters worse because I angled different this time with both hands free. The corner of the steel table connected with Rod's eye. There was no *clang*, no *bong*, no *crunch*. Just a horrible squishing sound.

In a crazed thrust, Rod, with his bloodied eye, grabbed both of my shoulders and yanked me to my right, his left. The top of my head cracked against the leg of the steel bench, and suddenly, I was no longer protected by a table or anything else. We were back to open space. Rod just held me down by my wrists at this point, like he'd given up any real effort to hurt me. Rod's knees were sprawled out to either side of me with all of his weight on top of me. Both of my hands were pinned above my head. I could feel the pounding of his heartbeat—and I mean *pounding*—against my lower belly and pelvis, where his femoral artery was pressed against me.

In a flash, I panicked—this dude was about to have a heart attack! And I was going to be charged with murder!

Suddenly, four officers burst into the dorm, pulling out their cans of pepper spray and stuck the cans in our faces.

"Break it up! Stop fighting now, or we're going to spray you both!"

"I can't get up with him on top of me," I gasped. "Get this fat ass off me!"

"Let him go, Huggins. Let him go and get off of him now!"

"No," said Rod, "if I let him go, he's going to hurt me."

"Do not hurt him when he lets go, inmate. Do you understand?"

"I don't *want* to hurt him, I just want his fat ass off of me."

"Huggins, he said he's not gonna hurt you. Now stand up and let him go."

"But I can't get up," Rod said. "I can't feel my legs. Please help me up"

Two of the officers grabbed Rod under the arms, one on each side. They stumbled backward trying to get him to the sitting position on the steel bench. As I stood up, one of the officers kept the pepper spray pointed in my face while the other one yanked my right and left arms behind my back and slapped on the cuffs. As I was turned around to face the vestibule at the entrance to the dorm, I saw one of the guards pulling out a video camera.

What the fuck did they need a video camera for? There are security cameras throughout the prison.

The officers didn't say anything as they escorted me to medical. Upon arrival, I was ordered to sit on an exam table while one of the guards stood in the doorway with the camera pointed at me. While I was waiting for the nurse to arrive, I wrinkled my nose. What was that putrid smell? I started looking around to try to see what smelled like shit, but I saw nothing in the room that explained it. I looked down at myself, and I realized that there was fecal matter smeared along my thighs and crotch as well as some clumped up on the bottom of my shirt.

"He shit on me!" I exclaimed. "Dude freaking shit on me! This is disgusting. Excuse me, officer, is there any chance that I can get a clean uniform? This is not hygienic."

The guard remained silent while holding the camera, but he wrinkled his face in disgust and turned his head to the side as if that would somehow protect him from contamination. He shook his head, then started shaking, struggling to contain his laughter so as to not have it recorded.

The nurse came in, an older white lady in her late sixties or early seventies. She was short but slender. We'd had prior interactions, and I knew for a fact I was not going to get any medical attention for anything from her—she was a straight-up white supremacist, not unusual for Citrus County, and on more than one occasion had said aloud that she thought Hitler was a great man, a brilliant man, and that someone should finish what he started.

"You look fine, boy. Why are you here? There's nothing wrong with you," she said. She turned to the guard. "He's fine. Get him out of here. I have to go do paperwork on the other one. They're going to remove what's left of his eye."

Soon I was guided to a holding cell with nothing but an empty three-by-six-foot metal bunk and a stainless steel toilet, still cuffed, still covered in shit. The guard turned off his stupid camera and left.

"Hey! Is someone going to uncuff me!" No response. I kicked the door like a bucking donkey.

"Knock it off, inmate! We will get to you when we get to you."

One thing prison does for you: it grants you long empty hours to reflect on the past should you choose to turn it over and over in your mind and *try* to figure out what went wrong. On my lonely bunk, during the hot, dreary afternoons, I lay there and wondered.

To the outside world, I didn't have a bad childhood. In fact, most people would think I had a perfect childhood with an awesome relationship with my parents and sisters. During my incarceration,

I was told many times that I was born with a silver spoon in my mouth. I never quite understood how that statement applied to me, although I can understand how poor, uneducated men who have never met their dads could think this.

But all so-called good childhoods are not created equal. As for mine, my parents never stopped reminding me that I was the problem child and that my sister was the one they loved most. Without a doubt, I had a temper, and I didn't always know how to control it. When I was eight years old, I got kicked out of YMCA summer camp because I threw a rock at a kid who had been bullying me, but I hit a different kid in the head. Well, I was eight years old, and my aim sucked.

When Dad picked me up, he wouldn't say a word to me. I wanted him to tell me he was proud of me for standing up to a bully, but he would not even look at me. When we got home, he took everything out of my room—I mean everything: my drawers, toys, clothing, pillows, furniture, even bedding. I was left with a mattress and the clothing I was wearing. I was allowed out in the morning for breakfast and to use the toilet, and then in the evening for the same. And I was eight years old. This solitary confinement lasted for a week.

At nine, I pushed my sister out of the way so I could brush my teeth before school. She had been in the bathroom staring at herself for nearly an hour, and I didn't want to miss the bus. She screamed and started crying. My parents knew that my sister could cry on command without any reason to—in fact, it was a source of entertainment at parties and gatherings. Even still, my father took off his belt and beat my ass for ten minutes. When I went to school, some of the bruises were visible on the back of my legs below my shorts line. The school counselor made me get naked in her office to examine the bruises.

This was more traumatic than the beating.

At ten years old, my mother shipped me off to Eckerd Youth Alternatives. It was a program for criminal teens to avoid prison. She told herself and others that she sent her ten-year-old son to live in the woods with a bunch of older criminal teens so that she could get a vacation from her problem child. What she really did was send me away so that she could dismantle the home and the family without opposition or guilt. I returned home to find that she'd cancelled all my father's credit cards, cleared out the joint bank accounts and safety deposit boxes, filed for divorce, and kicked my dad out of the house. He was staying in a roach motel trading IT work for rent as a result.

I had returned to a broken home. In no time, my mother started using me as a weapon to hurt my father. She would encourage my sisters to stand out front of the house, screaming, "All or none!"

I wanted to spend time with my dad, but my sisters made such a scene that I was not allowed to see my father, and he didn't get to see his children. All I wanted was to spend time with my dad.

One weekend when my sisters felt cooperative, we went to the beach with my father. We got carried away with the fun at the beach and needed to shower all the sand off before returning to mom's house. Still in bathing suits, we rinsed off the salt and sand in the shower two at a time. When my mother found out, she filed a complaint with the Department of Children and Families on the grounds that my father was allowing or encouraging sexually inappropriate behavior between his children. DCF did a huge investigation and determined that nothing untoward was occurring, but the investigation was traumatic nonetheless. The irony was that a few years later there would be sexual trauma and I'd be the one who ended up getting molested—in my mother's home, with her tacit knowledge and consent.

My mom had this crazy habit. When she knew I was packed to see my dad, she'd make me wait outside for him for hours before he'd show—sometimes as long as five hours just like after school. Meanwhile, my three younger sisters would be just on the other side of the door in the air-conditioned living room, watching television, drinking their sodas, and munching their snacks. There I'd sit, isolated and miserable, in 100 percent humidity and ninety-nine-degree weather, waiting and waiting and waiting and waiting. Which is why, even as an adult, I have an instant panic attack if I am ever locked out of my home.

But what inspired her cruelty? It's hard to say. My mother demanded perfection, from me especially. A 99.7% grade would get me grounded. A college-level essay would be marked up in red pen, to be rewritten over and over. Strangely, with my sisters, she didn't share this perfectionism. They could get seventies and walk off scot-free.

For me, it was perfection or punishment.

When I entered high school at twelve years old, my eleven-year-old sister, Naomi, had already discovered boys and pornography. I had not, and I had no interest in sex or romance. I was innocent and focused on academics, mostly because it's what mom expected. One day when I came home from school, my two youngest sisters didn't get home from elementary school for an hour and a half after we did. Naomi opened the glass sliding door one day and said, "Josh, I will let you inside the house until the bus gets here for Maggie and Monika if you don't tell Mom or anyone. But you must sit on the couch and watch television with me."

This was a no-brainer. Of course, I would watch TV in the air-conditioned house with food and snacks, even if it was only for an hour or so. Little did I know, she wanted to sit on the couch and watch porn together.

The first time we watched, I didn't know quite what I was seeing exactly, but I knew that it made my body do weird things that felt good but made me uncomfortable at the same time. I didn't say anything to anyone about it because I hated being locked outside so much that I didn't want to ruin my chance to stay inside. My sister was much more charismatic and confident than me. She was popular and influential. Unfortunately, Naomi turned that on me, and sitting next to each other eventually turned into more.

"Josh," she said the next time, "I want to see what happens to boys when they watch porn. Take your pants off and sit next to me."

"No!" I exclaimed. "That's gross! You are *my sister!*"

"If you don't," Naomi replied, "I will tell mom you forced your way into the house and made me watch you touch yourself."

I was an innocent kid, and I really didn't even understand that this was manipulation. I thought the threat was real, and, anyway, I knew that my parents would believe anything and everything Naomi said. I reluctantly complied, and as the situation progressed, I found myself being molested almost every day as a "science experiment." I knew it was wrong. It *felt* wrong. But I was more scared of what my parents would do to me if I spoke up than what would happen if I went along with it. I did protest and tell my sister I didn't want to do many things, and always ended up being coerced with the same threat that she would tell our mother that I was forcing her to do the very things she was forcing me to do.

I was stuck.

That is, until my mom came home early one day and found me in my underwear, tied to a chair with jump ropes—she'd caught my sister red-handed, molesting me—there was no two ways about it.

You would think that a mother would be shocked, that there would be screaming or consequences. Not so.

Instead, my mom got her camera and took a picture. For the next ten years, every time I ever brought a friend or girlfriend home for dinner or just to hang out, Mom would pull out the picture and show it to them with a story about how adorable it was that I let my sister tie me to a chair naked and put my hair in pigtails. My mother knew full well that the picture was a reminder of what had happened to me. She also knew there was nothing innocent about it.

A few days after the picture was taken, I packed all my belongings, put them on the front porch, called my father, and told him to come get me. I was moving in with him no matter what. The threat of telling Mom a lie that I was forcing her to do these things no longer held any power. There was no longer any reason to stay and endure the molestation, and I didn't feel like spending my life on the patio in the heat. I had lost all respect for my mother. I knew she didn't love me. And I wanted to be somewhere safe.

Dad was safe, or so I thought.

My parents were still in family court. Mom had convinced herself that because my father was a Jew, he had millions of dollars hidden away somewhere. Once I moved in with him, she lost a large portion of her control, because my sisters would come visit him to spend time with me. The all-or-none routine was done. Now she needed to find some other way to hurt my father.

Mom filed a complaint to DCF again that Dad was allowing sexually inappropriate relations between me and my sisters. DCF investigated again and again determined that there was nothing going on that they could verify, even when I told them what had happened that caused me to flee my mother's home. They confirmed what I already knew, that I had been a victim of sexual abuse, but they said there was nothing they could do about it since I'd already been removed from the situation and it was no longer ongoing. I didn't even tell my father the truth about what had happened. DCF dismissed me, so what could he do?

Unfortunately for me, my mother is a master manipulator and a narcissist. She convinced my sisters that I had been molesting them, and the two youngest were so young as to only remember what they were told. They grew up believing and telling my dad and anyone who would listen that I had molested them. In fact, their stories were all identical, identical to the things that had been done to me, except listing me as the perpetrator. All the family on my mom's side shunned me and abused me for years because of the stories that my sisters were telling, to the point that I stopped making any effort to attend family functions.

If there was any truth to their allegations, why didn't my mother ever send them to therapy? Why didn't my mother ever press charges? Why didn't my mother ever prohibit me from attending holidays or events with the family? Why didn't my mother ever prevent me from spending time with my sisters? Because she didn't want the truth that she allowed her son to be molested to see the light of day. Plain and simple.

In the holding cell, these memories would come like crashing waves for what felt like hours. Sterile white fluorescent lights and concrete walls made it difficult to have any perception of time of day or of the passage of time. All I knew was that my hands were asleep because the cuffs had cut off circulation before they even put me in the cell.

The chief of security appeared in the small plexiglass window and said, "What happened, inmate?"

I looked him directly in his eyes, making no effort to hide the hatred that I felt toward him. This man who had intercepted all of my letters to my attorney and read them, who had sat me down at the table in front of all the other guards with all the private letters I wrote to my attorney *open in his hand* to tell me that he was going to make sure I never reported what they were doing to me, this man has the gall to ask me what happened?

"Sir," I said, "I've got nothing to say to you. It's your job to know what has happened. I'm just an inmate. So if you have questions, do your job. I'm not doing it for you."

I turned around, walked across the small space of the cell, and sat down on the bunk. The chief of security was saying something, but the words didn't even register as I had already tuned him out.

Eventually, two of the guards arrived and escorted me from medical to confinement. It was the same damn dorm I'd already been in, but two cells down. Late in the afternoon, the guards brought Rod in to confinement and put him in the cell next to me. He had a patch over his eye and was wearing the same dirty clothes.

"Are you OK?" I asked.

"I'm good, man," Rod said. "My bad this morning. Blood sugar was low. Did you say anything to the police?"

"No," I said. "Except I told him to do his own damn job."

"A'ight," Rod said. "Pretty much what I told them too."

For the next several weeks, this was where I sat, alongside the man I'd almost blinded, a man so bighearted that he instantly forgave me. My fifteen months in jail had been, without question, the worst period in my life—a time so ugly I was certain, in fact, that life *could not be* any worse.

And then one morning the prison bus picked me up and took me to Century Correctional Facility, a place that was much, much worse.

DEATH WARRANT

Even after I'd been in custody for a couple of months, I was still sure I could beat the fictional narrative created by Derek Wallace. After all, the truth always comes out. The truth always wins, right?

What I didn't yet understand is that the reason the feds have a 97 percent conviction rate is not because they always catch the bad guy or even have substantial evidence. The reason the feds prevail is because they have created a law that eliminates the burden of proof. Despite my situation, I understood why they had created such a law. After all the years they'd spent chasing Al Capone, knowing all they knew about his many murders and crimes, they still could not *prove* anything until he made a mistake on his taxes. They needed "conspiracy," that catch-all charge created as part of the RICO (Racketeer Influenced and Corrupt Organizations) Act of the 1970s.

Of course, I was not part of an organized crime syndicate, or even a local gang. Hell, I was not even in any clubs. I worked, watched Netflix, didn't drink, didn't smoke, had never done any drugs, not even weed. The worst thing I had ever done—cheating on my cheating wife—was not exactly a criminal charge.

Derek Wallace pushed for conspiracy to commit fraud, all because I had not yet notified the VA to adjust my disability compensation two months after a divorce. It seems like a pittance, but this was the charge that would allow him to get a conviction without any evidence. It was also the charge that allowed him to roll out his fictional narrative, all about "a dishonest fraudster scamming honest taxpayers and veterans."

My attorney, Yvonne Gray, had made it clear to me that I *could* take it to trial and fight it, but because of the nature of the conspiracy charge, I would inevitably lose—they simply didn't need to prove anything. Take any charge and put the words "conspiracy to commit" in front of it and the feds can use it with impunity. It's the ultimate back-up option.

I didn't care. I was determined to have my day in court, even after Derek Wallace showed up at my parents' home in Boca Raton with a search warrant to obtain my computer. My father had traveled to Hollywood, Florida, to pack up all of my belongings after the arrest. Of course, my parents complied without hesitation and handed over my computer—but Wallace wasn't satisfied. He insisted that he needed to search their home, and despite my parents protests, he tore through their bedrooms and kitchen, closets and cabinets. Then he wanted search my stepmother's jewelry box for absolutely no good reason. My stepmom, Joselyn, a woman with multiple PhDs who'd raised two children alone, stood him down and forced him out of her house.

Wallace didn't stop with my family—he harassed every person he could at Candlewood Community Church, all my friends and colleagues from Venice, Sarasota, Hollywood, Tampa, and Boca, including former employers, professors, teachers, and family. He was on a mission, doing everything he could to intimidate them, threatening their professional standing to find something, anything, he could to hurt me. He showed up in the hospital where my father was a respected biomedical engineer. He showed up on University of South Florida campus where my mentor, Steve, was a professor of architecture. He showed up at the food pantry where I had volunteered. Then he told my landlord that my service dog—prescribed by a VA doctor, no less—was not a real service dog. It didn't take long before I was evicted.

My attorney strongly recommended that I extend a proffer, and so I decided that I would plead guilty to this ridiculous fifty-seven-dollar crime that I had not committed, in the hopes that it would mean that law enforcement would finally stop bothering people I cared about. Truth was, I didn't even really know what *proffer* meant, but once I found out it amounted to snitching on others. I started unloading everything I knew about Wallace, all the illegal things he had done. The Assistant US District Attorney was not interested in hearing about the wrongdoing of a law enforcement officer or anyone else with a badge. Outside Wallace and his crew, though, there really wasn't anything I could tell them. I didn't know any criminals, I myself was not a criminal, and I tended to surround myself with people who were straightlaced, kindhearted, and even a little nerdy.

And so I took the hit—a full fifteen-month sentence. I showed up to court in blue scrubs. Everything was always blue. Blue pants, blue shirt with a pocket on the breast, blue undershorts, black crocks. My feet were shackled, and my hands were cuffed, and as if that was not sufficient to protect all the armed guards, my handcuffs were chained to my foot shackles. I was kept in a cement holding cell that was all blue and gray. Wallace stopped in to gloat, this time wearing a US Marshals bulletproof vest. Everyday pretending to be someone he is not, huh? He even told me that as he had spent so much time getting to know me, in another life we could have been friends. How insulting is that?

When I was brought into the courtroom, it was extremely quiet, dark-wood paneling on the walls and high ceiling, dark orangish-brown carpeting that looked like it was straight out of the 1970s, and of course, about ten feet above the floor perched the judge in her flowing black robes. The term *presiding* is apt, as the entire scene reminded me of a king sitting on her throne, looking down upon the filthy commoners in disgust. There were even spectators, just like in the Dark Ages. There was a reporter, a bunch of lawyers, and a slender woman in dark, high-necked professional attire looking angry at me. My father was present, but he was the only support I had.

I sat next to Yvonne, and once the judge was situated, she gave Yvonne an opportunity to advocate for a slap on the wrists. Nearly everything she said was opposed by the Assistant US District Attorney, who was seated next to Wallace. When Yvonne finished asking for the minimum and explaining all the reasons why such as ties to the community, military service, intentions, disabilities, and so on, the ADA had her say. She was nasty, aggressive woman, wearing a gray power suit, her hair tightly bound into a bun. She was sharp and intense with her words, and she made sure that Wallace had a chance to present his entire narrative to the judge, despite Yvonne vehemently protesting that it was not relevant. Wallace had requested the five-year maximum because I was "so dangerous," and Yvonne requested that I get released on probation because that is what I realistically qualified for, based on the charges and my lack of a criminal record.

Judge Veronica Huntington decided arbitrarily that a compromise meant eighteen months behind bars, only serving fifteen months if I behaved myself. The slender woman in the dark outfit made noises every time Yvonne said something positive about me or about why I did not deserve a huge period of incarceration. I got the feeling that she was either connected to Wallace or connected to Maddie in some way. To this day, I have no idea who she was, but she clearly hated me with a passion and was very pleased when I was given the eighteen-month prison sentence.

Naturally, it blew me away that taking someone's freedom could be so subjective and arbitrary, but I also felt devastated. I was terrified of prison, crushed that I was going to lose everything: my apartment that I had prepaid a year on, my motorcycle, my students and reputation as a martial arts instructor. I knew that all of my military and government contracts were done. Never again would I be allowed on to MacDill Air Force Base to teach special operations. Everything that I had spent years building, gone in an instant, at the arbitrary whim of a fellow human. There was a sensation that a giant hole had been ripped open in my stomach and chest, that there was cold emptiness where my life and soul used to be.

There was nothing to do but wait it out at Citrus Detention Facility until they figured out where to send me. For two weeks, the staff refused to give me my prescribed meds—Paxil and morphine—and stopping cold turkey could cause serious harm. I had been prescribed morphine by the Department of Veterans Affairs for the three ruptured disks in my back sustained during military service, and the Paxil was for severe anxiety and PTSD. I was shaking and sweating, experiencing random brain zings, a common and horrific side effect of Paxil, sick as a dog. Then came the lockdown, two days confined to our cells while the staff did some major shakedown, in search of who knows what.

One afternoon a door buzzed, and I sat up as it swung open. My roommate Pedro didn't speak English, but he knew the smell of food and the words "chow time." He was here because the Baez brothers paid his family a million dollars to deliberately get caught with a boat of cocaine. They "proffered" information regarding his location and paid his family for him to voluntarily get caught and arrested. The ten years he was serving would take ten years off the sentences of the cartel leaders who had paid him to take the fall. Crazy, but that's how it works.

Desperate for my meds, I took advantage of the open door and ducked my six-foot three-inch, 265-pound frame under the arms of the guard serving the chow and made a run for the main door to the cellblock.

"Hey," the guard shouted, "get back here!"

I ignored him and headed straight for the door. There was a little silver button on the wall by the main door, with a silver speaker grill above it. I started pressing the button frantically, over and over again.

A woman's voice crackled out of the speaker. "Yes, inmate?"

"I need my medication," I said. "I haven't had my meds in two weeks, and I am having serious medical issues. Please get someone down here—*please!*"

The woman started speaking, but I didn't hear anything else as the main door buzzed open, and a man in blue jeans and a Pittsburgh Steelers cap walked in.

"Please tell them to give me my medication!" I begged him.

Without responding, he slammed the heel of his palm into my chest, right where my heart was, putting all of his body weight into the strike. I think he was trying to turn me around so he could re-strain me, but he was about a hundred pounds lighter than me, and I had spent most of the last five years training and teaching Krav Maga to military and intelligence personnel, full-time, and so, without really trying, I didn't budge.

His eyes widened just slightly, and he shoved me again. Again, I didn't budge when he struck me. He balled his hand into a fist and slammed it into my face, and once again, his eyes widened as I barely moved despite him hitting me solidly on the jaw. Why was he so driven to force things to escalate? He wasn't. He just didn't care, because guards have absolute power and no oversight. What would have helped defuse the situation? Only my absolute submission and compliance, which was not an option. I'm certainly not saying he wasn't a scumbag (he was actually not one of the bad ones), but something about that moment went way overboard. The guards were all assholes, but in the big picture he was one of the nicer ones. It may have been my demeanor, or that he had a fight with his wife, or anything else that made him behave out of character at that moment. I will never know.

By the second strike to my face, I'd had enough. Maybe I deserved the first punch, but if I were to let him hit me three times, I was asking to be a victim, and so, as he moved to hit me again, I jabbed him in the stomach with my left hand, causing him to nearly double over at the waist. I shifted my weight to the left, turning my hips slightly, and pushed from my right foot through to the ceiling. I snapped my right hand up, keeping my elbow tight by my ribs. The uppercut smashed into his jaw, and my upward force was amplified by his downward momentum, just like the math problem where the two trains collide, each moving at sixty mph with the combined 120 impact.

His hands dropped to protect his jaw, but I was already snapping back to the right to slam my left fist into the orbit of his right eye. I connected and felt something break. Both of his hands jerked up, as if to grab the back of his head and protect his temples, leaving his jaw perilously exposed. I hit him in the same spot on his jaw with the same angle and force. Both of his hands jerked down to protect his jaw again. I exploded with my left fist into the orbit of his eye, same target as before and at exactly the same angle.

In that moment of desperation, there was a part of me that wanted to hurt him, to break him the way I was being broken, to take something from him that I could not put into words, his sense of security maybe, as was being done to me. In that moment, I needed him to *feel* the intensity of what I was experiencing, as all of my words had fallen on deaf ears. I hit him with everything I had, and the damage revealed that. He did not deserve what I did, as I did not deserve what happened to me. As skilled as I am, absolutely I could have grappled with him or done something else. However, given that I was experiencing massive psychiatric and physical withdrawals from being denied access to medication that *absolutely cannot* be stopped cold turkey, I do not think that I had the mental wherewithal to think that clearly. I was in a primal survival mentality.

We did this dance three times, three hits to the jaw, three to the eye. After the sixth hit, I realized that he was not making any aggressive moves anymore. He was just holding his head, curled into a standing fetal position.

"Get down, motherfucker!" the officer who was passing out chow screamed. "Get on the ground!" He was walking toward me as fast as his immense girth allowed while pulling out his pepper spray canister. Meanwhile, the other officer who was helping with the chow was running toward me, also pulling out pepper spray. They both got to me at about the same time, one directly in front and the other off to my right about forty-five degrees. Both of them managed to keep the stainless steel tables between me and them. They unloaded their canisters of paper spray and CS gas directly into my face. Not just a little bit either—these were two-liter bottles spraying streams directly in my mouth and eyes.

I started walking toward the officers to stop them, still perplexed. I had been begging for medical help when this random guard assaulted me, hit me three times before I made any effort to defend myself. Now I was being attacked again. I got a couple of steps in, and I suddenly found myself flying through the air. Then the ground slammed into me. I slipped in the puddle of pepper spray that had pooled on the ground from them spraying me and found myself lying in it.

Before I could even process what had happened, both officers were standing over me and spraying everything that was left in their cans directly into my eyes, nose, and mouth from inches away.

"Stop struggling!" one of them shouted.

I felt something explode in my groin and realized that a grown man had dropped all of his weight onto my balls. I cried out in pain and got a mouthful of paper spray and CS gas.

"Stop struggling!" the guard shouted again.

Suddenly, there were four officers, and they were all kneeling on me while twisting my wrists and arms in directions they were never meant to go. I was forced over onto my belly, face down in the puddle of chemical irritants.

"Stop struggling!" he shouted a third time.

Two men had their knees in the small of my back, right on the injured disks and damaged portion of my spine. One man had his knee on my testicles and seemed to be deliberately trying to pop them under his weight.

"Stop struggling!" another guard shouted.

But I wasn't struggling. Is this what they are told to say so that they can always cover their ass? I felt the cold bite of handcuffs on my wrists and then the sharp pain as the cuffs were overtightened, cutting into the nerves of my hands and wrists.

"Stop struggling!"

I tried to speak, but I was face down in a pool of chemicals. I tried to lift my face to breathe, but I had my head slammed into the concrete by one of the guards.

"Stop struggling!"

I tried to breathe air instead of liquid and got punched in the face right before having my head shoved back down into the chemical puddle.

"Stop struggling!"

All of a sudden, my eyes were on fire, my nose and throat were burning, and I couldn't breathe. Mucus gushed from my nose and mouth, cutting off the last of my breath. The pepper spray and the CS gas were interacting—it took just a little while to affect me because I had a big tolerance for pain, but now I was going down, crippled, maybe dying.

I felt myself being lifted up by the handcuffs as two of the guards grabbed me from either side, putting their arms under and through my handcuffed arms, grabbing me by the back of my collar.

Bent over at the waist, hands cuffed behind my back, and pulled up toward the ceiling, I was dragged by the officers in this contorted position to the medical portion of the facility. It felt like miles of hallway, with multiple turns and twists, with the guards practically running, my toes dragging on the ground behind me.

"Do we have to let him rinse his eyes?" Officer Farquaad asked the nurse in his heavy Boston accent.

"I just watched you give him two minutes at the eye wash," the nurse responded. I couldn't see her, but she sounded like an angry grandmother.

"Sounds good," Farquaad responded.

"I cannot see!" I screamed. "I can't breathe, and my eyes are burning!"

"You can breathe just fine," the nurse said sharply. "If you couldn't breathe, you wouldn't be able to speak. Now get him out of here."

Down dozens of hallways and many turns, I was finally thrown into a holding cell. It was empty, nothing but a cement floor and a steel toilet. I remained on the floor of this room where I landed when they threw me in. I cried, but my tears reactivated the chemical compounds on my face, and within seconds, my eyes were burning at full intensity, my nose pouring mucus through a thick cough.

"You ah fine!" Officer Farquaad shouted in his thick Boston accent. "Keep it down!"

They kept the lights on and studiously ignored me, so I had no concept of the passage of time, but it felt like days before there was even an acknowledgment of my existence.

Suddenly, there was a commotion outside of my door. I got up and went over, peering out of the small window to see what the excitement was about.

"He shattered the guard's face," Captain Bowman, a very large, dark-haired woman, was saying. "He shattered both orbits on his eyes, shattered his upper and lower jaw on both sides, shattered his nose, collapsed his tear ducts, and collapsed his sinuses. Gonna need major reconstructive surgery."

"This asshole signed his own death warrant," Farquaad replied. "He hurt one of ours, and we never walk alone."

MADDIE

Prior to meeting her, my romantic history was sparse: just one significant relationship back in high school, sprinkled with few fleeting intimacies. As a bookworm and an introvert, I was far from the kind of guy who caught girls' attention. My mother and sisters rarely showed me affection, leaving a gaping void in my heart—a yearning to matter, to be loved by a woman.

Then came Maddie, a breathtaking amalgamation of Italian and Lebanese heritage, an embodiment of beauty that surpassed any woman I had ever met. Her gentle and melodious voice, her quiet and introverted disposition, her apparent obliviousness to her own beauty, all made her stand out as a unique gem. She was an absolute beauty, a twelve on a ten-point scale. Upon setting my eyes on her, I was irrevocably smitten.

Without a second thought, I plunged into the sea of trust, love, and devotion. She was six months younger than me, and objectively out of my league. Yet, in a blink, she had my heart captive, and soon we found ourselves sharing a home. "I only have eyes for you"—a cliché for most, but for me, an undeniable truth. Every moment with Maddie was like an eternal honeymoon, a whirlwind of passion, desire, and laughter. Even moments of tranquility carried their own enchantment. I would have gladly spent every second by her side, reveling in her company.

But, alas, I was a fool.

"Nothing, it's nothing!" Maddie cried out, her face flushed with anger and disbelief, her right hand clenched into a fist and her left one gripping her cell phone tightly. She was in her Daiquiri Deck tank top and shorts—the attire for her job at the restaurant where she didn't work that day. I knew because I had gone there for lunch and asked for her. Now, I was stammering, struggling to spit out my words as my chest and throat tightened and my tongue seemed to twist into knots.

"I trusted you!" I managed to utter. "I love you! Why would you pretend to go to work, then head to a hotel and rack up a seventy-eight-dollar bill in the middle of the afternoon?"

"Josh, I did go to work, but they sent me back because they were slow. Adam was waiting at my car, and he wouldn't leave unless I agreed to have lunch with him. That bill was for lunch," she protested.

I kept my cool, leveraging my training as a US Marine. But it was clear as day: she was having an affair, and the suspicious stain on the back seat of her car was a damning testament.

Abruptly, Maddie announced, "I want to move to Tampa. There's a campus of the University of South Florida there. And with

Adam not having a car, he won't be able to bother me as it's an hour drive north."

The sudden switch in the conversation's course caught me off guard. Looking back, I realize now that Maddie was a master manipulator, always a step ahead in her cunning plans.

"I love you, Josh," she continued, her voice sweet and persuasive. "If we move, Adam won't be an issue anymore. He doesn't have a car. Plus, with my schoolwork and studying for the GRE, I'll be too busy to entertain any distractions. Please, Josh." Her innocent plea had me falling for her tricks once again.

Fast-forward to my birthday a few weeks later. Our move to Tampa was imminent, our belongings mostly packed except for the waterbed. But that day was about me. Maddie, who was supposed to work the evening shift, came home at an unusually late 3:30 a,m. I was ready for a confrontation about her tardiness, assuming Adam was involved again. But she walked in with a box in her hands, serenading me with a "Happy Birthday" and a kiss. She apologized for her lateness and explained she had stopped to get me a pie from Perkins. It wasn't my favorite, as I disliked lemon meringue, but the gesture moved me, and I appreciated the effort.

We spent my birthday in blissful intimacy—she made me breakfast in bed. We enjoyed each other's company, made love, watched *The Hitchhiker's Guide to the Galaxy*, strolled along the beach, and feasted on wings and beers at Bogey's Grill. However, halfway through a movie later in the day, I noticed her phone buzzing incessantly with texts. I asked her about it, and she brushed it off, saying it was a former coworker. We ended the night sipping artisan beers at a wine bar near our home, before heading back and continuing the celebration with a game of Truth, Dare, Drink.

I woke up the next day with a throbbing headache and blurry memories. Maddie was sleeping peacefully while a duffel bag stuffed with socks and sweatshirts sat by the front door, the remnants of my drunken antics the night before. As I pieced together the events, I spotted Maddie's phone on the coffee table. Overcome by curiosity, I decided to snoop into her messages. The so-called friend she had been texting turned out to be Adam. The threads of betrayal began to unravel, and reality crashed down on me like a ton of bricks:

> *Josh is such a stupid, arrogant, idiot. He is sitting right next to you in the theater on his birthday, and you are paying more attention to me than to him, and he thinks you are talking to a girlfriend. He doesn't even suspect that it's me.*

Throughout the day, she had been in constant communication with him, providing a play-by-play of our activities, voicing her longing for his presence. He, in turn, asked if I had discovered the incriminating white stain on the backseat of her car, and they began to orchestrate their next clandestine rendezvous. The pain of the unfolding betrayal was staggering. Despite my shock, I was held captive by fear—the fear of losing her. The possibility of finding another woman as brilliant and as beautiful who would notice someone like me seemed near impossible. Maddie was leagues above me, and I couldn't stand the thought of losing her.

The only viable solution appeared to be the relocation.

Our migration to Tampa needed to happen sooner than planned. In fact, it needed to happen immediately.

The relocation process was seamless. We found a charming, one-bedroom apartment located within walking distance of Busch Gardens and the University of South Florida Campus. Our new home was nestled in a pleasant neighborhood, conveniently situated near Maddie's university where she intended to complete her undergrad.

In an odd sense, life was remarkable. We were sharing our first apartment together—a clean, beautiful space with solid walls that encouraged unrestrained passion. Together, we delved into the thrill of exploring Tampa, a refreshingly romantic experience. Adam, fortunately, was handicapped by multiple DUI charges and therefore lacked a driver's license, which made the hour-long distance between him and us a considerable barrier. I finally felt a wave of relief wash over me. Adam was no longer a looming threat. There was no more cheating, no more distrust, and most importantly, no more jealousy. Maddie had plunged herself into a full course load at USF, juggling six classes alongside her new job at the local Applebee's up the road.

I occupied my time with a part-time gig at the Pub in the Tampa International Mall, a British pub with a unique dress code requiring men to wear kilts. However, my ultimate goal was to establish my own business here teaching Krav Maga and Jujitsu. To do this, I had to navigate the catch-22 of needing customers to afford a facility but needing a facility to attract customers. Thankfully, I found a solution. Leveraging Maddie's student status, I discovered I could utilize USF's extensive athletic facilities for free if I could persuade a few students to establish a free student organization.

Thus began my journey of teaching Krav Maga and Jujitsu under the pavilion on the Fowler Ave soccer/football fields, directly across from the Museum of Science and Industry. At first, my only student was Maddie. Gradually, more students, intrigued by our activities, joined our ranks. Among them were Robert—a stereotypical college gym rat with an extraordinary knack for physical learning—and David, Robert's brother, who was preparing for army basic training. The two of them played crucial roles in advertising our training sessions across campus.

Before long, my roster grew to include a nurse in her forties, a young musician, and a feisty eighteen-year-old named Monika, who had just enlisted in the national guard. These steadfast individuals weathered each day, braving Florida's unpredictable weather and challenging training regimens. Their determination led to an opportunity for me to train over a hundred disciplined students during the Florida Army National Guard's training weekend.

Life was at its peak—I was in love, building a real business, and making a difference in these young lives. What could possibly go wrong?

POLICE IMPERSONATORS

Life was at an all-time high, and the work was coming in faster than I could book it. The national guard met to train one weekend per month and two weeks during the summer, so month after month, Maddie, I, and a few of my students loaded up and spent four hours teaching soldiers everything they needed to know about combat. Sometimes we taught them knife fighting techniques. Sometimes we trained them on firearm tactics. Often we trained them with unarmed moves like striking and grappling. On one occasion, we were able to get Major Jacob Ryan and Sergeant Ryan to unlock the armory, and we ran through some rifle and bayonet moves. Maddie usually accompanied me and took pictures and video, and I was proud to have her see me leading the charge.

Meanwhile, an unsettling reality was unfurling beneath the surface. The alarming news came from Sergeant Ryan that an agent from the Department of Veterans Affairs, Veteran Fraud Division, had started sniffing around. I was utterly confused—my morphine prescription for my knee and back injuries was legitimate and above-board. Nonetheless, there was nothing much I could do but wait and see what unfolded.

After Maddie's betrayal with Adam, I found solace in the companionship of an older couple I was training. They drew me into their world as swingers, providing a nonjudgmental space that made me feel valued and appreciated. My broken heart found comfort in these new experiences. I began seeking solace through intimate encounters with other married women or couples I met on Craigslist whenever Maddie's actions reopened old wounds. This form of therapy soon found its way into my professional life—about forty percent of my students were fit, attractive women, generally dominant and assertive.

Diamond, an enchanting doctor who came to my dojo for the first time in a blue minivan with dark-tinted windows, immediately caught my attention. After just three one-hour training sessions, we found ourselves entangled on the mats in the empty dojo under the pretext of an extra lesson. But after that night, Diamond disappeared, never to return. However, this didn't bother me much, as I found myself uninterested in any other woman than Maddie after a single encounter.

About nine months before Sergeant Ryan's ominous discussion, around two weeks following my fleeting affair with Diamond, a blue minivan was parked in my reserved parking space in our apartment complex. An eruption of fury ignited within me as I noticed this invasion of my paid territory. Marching up to the driver's window, a hint of familiarity crossed my mind—this was Diamond's van! Through the darkened tint, the window lowered just enough to reveal the face of a man, not Diamond, but someone outfitted in a bulletproof vest emblazoned with the word POLICE.

I questioned him sharply, "Why have you parked in my spot?"

His unexpectedly amiable demeanor caught me off guard. Introducing himself as Derek Wallace, he explained he was a special investigator with the Pasco County Sheriff's Office, working on a human trafficking case. According to him, my parking spot offered the perfect vantage point to keep tabs on the nearby Hispanic church, the subject of their investigation. An apology for my rudeness slipped from my lips as he unfolded the dark tale of his mission—I was eager to contribute in any way toward defeating such a heinous crime.

What I failed to realize then was that Wallace was not an officer of the Pasco County Sheriff's Department or any other police department. The real "bad guy" he sought was me, but oblivious to his true intentions, I offered him unlimited access to the parking spot.

When the university's facilities were not available, I taught martial arts at my home garage and I often took a low dosage of government-prescribed morphine to manage the pain in order to teach effectively. Wallace, acting as a silent observer from his stakeout, must have found these sessions entertaining. Two months into his masquerade, he extended an invitation for me to train his military unit, claiming to be a major in the US Army Reserves 377th Military Intelligence Battalion.

Seeing this as a prestigious opportunity and potential path to lucrative government contracts, I eagerly agreed. So, my best team members—Conan, Monika, and Jon—and I packed our gear and set course to Orlando. The training seminar was a hit; we showcased combat techniques for potential prisoner-of-war situations and shared controlling techniques that used force without leaving traces. The success led to another invitation, to train the 317th Military Police Battalion in Tampa.

Wallace informed us about the impending annual budget review, promising to allocate a portion for our Academy of Krav Maga and Jujitsu. Our team was elated at the prospect of serving the US Army professionally, instead of volunteering.

However, a severe car accident soon disrupted the newfound excitement. A truck rear-ended me, causing a pile-up and wrecking Maddie's Honda Civic. A frantic search for Abby, my dog who was thrown from the car, ended in me collapsing on the ground, overwhelmed with grief.

My joy was restored when a kind stranger informed me they'd found Abby, yet the loss of the car and the impending physical trauma lingered. Days later, an intense fatigue and nausea overcame me. Attempting to find relief through rest, I woke to find myself paralyzed by an unbearable pain in my legs, unable to move.

Maddie, occupied with her classes, had advised me to call an ambulance. The arrival of the EMTs was made possible by Abby, who managed to open the locked front door on my command. Together, we were transported to the Bruce B. Downs VA Medical Center.

At the hospital, I was immediately taken for scans that revealed that the impact from the crash had aggravated the previously injured disks in my lower spine. On the fourth day, medical staff administered epidural and steroid injections. By the fifth day, I was gingerly navigating the hospital hallways and finally released the following afternoon.

* * *

I found myself discharged from the VA Medical Center on a frosty January afternoon, with an impending commitment to teach a fresh batch of army military police the following day. Despite my physical condition crying for rest, my sense of duty, paired with an inkling of excitement, propelled me to honor this commitment. I arrived on the scene, leaning heavily on a cane, candidly expressing my recent brush with surgery. The reins of teaching were firmly held by my team as I contributed from the sidelines, shouting necessary corrections and instructions. Despite our collective effort, our first impression left much to be desired. A follow-up call to schedule the next session was met with indifferent excuses, hinting at mandatory training before our addition to their curriculum. As the battalion and Sergeant Ryan went silent, a sense of unease crept in. Though class cancellations were not unheard of, this sudden shift felt peculiar.

At this point, what I didn't know was a dramatic revelation that could have spun my world out of control. Derek Wallace, the man who was supposed to be a partner in our endeavor, was a mere illusion. He was Diamond's husband and was fueled by a thirst for vengeance. His motive stemmed from our steamy past, his wife and me entangled in an affair. Rather than confronting me directly about it, he took an elaborate path, molding our classes into an intricate ruse. His aim was to paint me as a fraud, feigning disability while siphoning funds from the government.

Instead of resorting to physical confrontation or attempting an arrest, he exploited his government position, building a narrative over two years. His target wasn't some distant church but me, and the narrative was to be my downfall. Despite trailing me relentlessly, he couldn't find a shred of illegitimate activity to accuse me of, from minor infringements to serious crimes. So, he lay in wait for the perfect moment to strike.

The opportunity he yearned for arrived in the wake of heartache. Maddie, my beloved, married me for the sake of Florida residency, as her education was financed by her mother and she was paying inflated pricing as an out-of-state student. Once she graduated, she packed her things and proposed an amicable divorce. An agreement to restart our relationship on better terms masked the devastating blow. Despite the tumult of our relationship, I found myself clinging to the promise of a second chance. Unfortunately, in my desperation, I overlooked the legal obligation to inform the VA about the divorce in writing within thirty days.

Wallace pounced on this detail when he discovered it, filed criminal charges, and used the grand jury as a platform to spin a wild narrative—all about a despicable veteran pretending to be unable to walk while secretly teaching martial arts, "getting over" on the taxpayers. The fact that I hadn't yet reported this change was all he needed to nab the platform.

I wasn't charged with faking my disability, though that would have been heinous enough. I was charged with "conspiring to defraud the United States." This word *conspire* meant that no actual crime had been committed, only that I had made plans to commit a crime, frequently invoked as a provision of the RICO act to nail organized crime organizations. The Federal Government maintains their 99.7 percent conviction rate with the general conspiracy statute, 18 U.S.C. §371: "To conspire to defraud the United States means primarily to cheat the Government out of property or money, but it also means to interfere with or obstruct one of its lawful governmental functions by deceit, craft or trickery."

I had been overpaid by roughly $50 per month *for one month* since my divorce, but was ordered to pay back over $89K, the arbitrary amount Wallace determined that I would have received over the rest of my life, had I not been caught.

It has never been entirely clear to me how he managed to sell the story and make it plausible that anyone would somehow be smart enough to deceive countless doctors, surgeons, nurses, mental health providers, and physical therapists, manipulating X-rays and MRIs and the radiologists who reviewed those results in private.

It was bad enough that the marriage was ending. I was heartbroken, suicidal, just devastated. I could think of nothing but Maddie—and it wasn't like she was out of my life. We still talked on the phone every day, texted every day, had phone sex, flirted. After graduation in May, she moved back to Chicago. In October, I flew to visit her and we spent a long weekend together in my hotel room, making love and acting like a new couple, like everything was on the mend. In fact, we talked about rebuilding, starting over. She wanted a reboot—the normal courtship we'd never had the first time around, with a proper proposal and a wedding.

I agreed—a reboot was what we needed. A few weeks later, she came down to Florida and stayed in my apartment with me for another long, happy weekend—she sat in my lap and fed me breakfast, I cooked lunch and dinner for her, we walked on the beach holding hands, and she cried because of how much she had missed it all. It really felt like we were back in the honeymoon phase, even when she stayed with me in December to finalize the divorce—right up until the moment that they arrested me.

Here's the thing: a conspiracy charge requires two people. One cannot conspire all by one's lonesome. When Derek Wallace and his squad of heavily armored officers and SWAT teams arrested me, they also arrested Maddie. I don't know the details, but I did hear that her mother paid the federal government about $20,000 to purchase Maddie's freedom. She managed to not only avoid jail time but also any criminal conviction.

I sent her 1,752 letters during my five-year incarceration, roughly one letter per day. In my head and heart, she was still my wife. I was in love, and absence only made the heart grow fonder, the indiscretions fading and forgotten. We had been on track to rebuild, and I never let go of the hope that was still possible. She remained my wife in my heart, my love for her blossoming in the face of absence. Time seemed to stand still. My hope for our future together remained alive. For me, time stood still for five years. For the rest of the world, time moved on.

THE HOMICIDAL
ROOMMATE

Every day for almost fifty-six weeks after brawling with the guards, I got beaten to a pulp, even tortured, but it was the solitude that really killed. If I only had someone to talk to or a sip of water, I could survive. But with no water for weeks except for what was in the toilet, no food for weeks except for a slice of white bread every fourteen days, and no one to talk to but a little pet cockroach that I named Fred, I was unravelling. I wanted to die.

Why, I wondered, *won't they just kill me?* I'd begged them to end it many times already. I didn't have any tears left to cry, except for that scary time of day when I begged God to make it stop, begged God to have today be the day I wouldn't wake up from the beatings.

The only people they allowed me to speak to were my attorney, Anthony Silverstone, and Judge Howard. I knew when those talks were coming because the beatings would stop, always exactly two weeks before a court appearance or a lawyer's visit. The talks didn't do much good. Even after I told Judge Howard what had been happening to me, he was dismissive. "If that was really happening, somebody would've said something" was his stony reaction.

I got the gist: he didn't care.

My lawyer, Anthony Silverstone, cared, but there was nothing he could do. After all, how could I document my injuries? The guards stopped leaving marks two weeks before he came so that all the bruises and marks would have faded by visitation time. In a crazy attempt to make sure the bruises stayed fresh and the open cuts stayed open, I tried to beat myself. I would throw myself against the edge of the steel bunk in order to keep the bruises on my back, my shoulders, the backs of my legs and the backs of my arms fresh, keep the cuts open and bleeding. I cannot count the number of times I hit myself in the face in order to keep the wounds fresh, but as anyone who has genuinely attempted to harm themselves can attest, it is a war internally to override your natural aversion to pain and injury.

The forearms and the lower legs were easier to ensure that the wounds stayed fresh and visible until my attorney could take pictures. Those on my back and my face were much harder. You would think it would have been easy, but one of the most mentally challenging things I have ever done is slam my face into the corner of a steel bunk, targeting an infected wound to make sure it didn't heal before it could be witnessed.

My attorney had special privileges—he could bring a phone or an iPad as long as it left with him. I was going to get these monsters, I had to. It was the only thing that kept me going through the torture—the cold rage and absolute hatred for the people who were abusing me, especially Officer Green and Officer Farquaad. Although my burning fury and my desire for vengeance was powerful, the incredible hopelessness and the desire to end my suffering was still greater.

After roughly a year, I had resigned myself to the fact that this purgatory was hell and that I was stuck here. I couldn't end my life, as they made sure I didn't have access to anything that would accomplish such a task. They wouldn't kill me, because that would be too easy, and they wanted me to suffer. The dead do not suffer. The courts had no urgency to address my case, so there was no end in sight; I could be looking at thirty more years of this. The act of giving up—of total surrender—is not an instant thing. It is not a switch that suddenly flips, not something you suddenly decide. No, it is a slow decent into abject hopelessness, crossing through despair and grief until hope is slowly and imperceptibly extinguished. By the time you realize you are giving up, it has already happened. I do not know when it had happened, but it had. That made what came next so profound.

Boom! Boom! Boom!

A guard pounded on the door to my cell.

"Turn around and cuff up. You're getting a roommate!" the officer shouted through the slender flap where the food was passed through. I turned around and walked backward toward the door, bending over at the waist and squatting down as I extended my hands back through the food flap. The officer put on the handcuffs and overtightened them. He opened the door and grabbed me roughly by the back of my arm just above the elbow.

"Up against the wall!" he screamed as he shoved my face hard into the concrete block wall just inside the cell door.

"I'm cooperating. Is that really necessary?" I asked.

"Shut up and face the wall!" he shouted. I did as I was told. With my forehead pressed up against the white concrete wall, I stood there listening to the sounds of a mattress being dragged in, followed by the sounds of chains and shackles as another inmate shuffled into my box. I felt his arm brush against mine as he assumed the same position with his forehead against the wall and his feet spread as wide as the shackles would allow.

Con-con-con-con-chink!

The door slammed shut. We took turns repeating the process of backing up to the door, bending over at the waist and squatting down to put our hands through the bean flap. When I finally looked at this intruder into what little space I had, I saw a young, innocent-looking kid maybe nineteen years old, round cherub-shaped face with platinum-blond hair, maybe five feet four inches tall.

They'd put a child into the room with me.

"Hi! Name is Ben. What's going on?" he said as he extended his hand to shake mine. For a moment, I was confused. What did he want me to do with his hand? What did he want from me? Why was he standing there looking like he's waiting for something from me? Then it dawned on me. He wanted to shake my hand because that's how two humans introduce themselves. I had forgotten what it felt like to be treated like a person. As I shook his hand, blown away by the incredible sensation of nonaggressive contact, I introduced myself in turn.

"I'm Josh. What brings you to this shithole of a neighborhood?"

He looked at me like an innocent child with a slight smile on his face as he said nonchalantly, "Oh, I stabbed my mother and girlfriend to death. Then I forced my friend to help me hide the bodies."

"Are you serious? I think you're just pulling my leg. What are you really in for?"

Looking me square in the eyes, the most piercing blue eyes I had ever seen, he continued to tell me casually about what he'd done. "My girlfriend and I were camping out in a tent by the river, and my mom— she pissed me off for the last time. I pulled out my hunting knife, and

I stabbed her in the chest. My girlfriend wouldn't stop screaming even though I asked her really nicely to stop, so I stabbed her in the throat seven times. I had my friend come out to help me with the bodies, but then he went to the police and snitched on me. So now I'm here, and I've already been found guilty. I'm just waiting to find out whether I'm going to get the death penalty or life in prison."

What. The. Fuck.

I had broken the nose of an off-duty correctional officer in self-defense. For my trouble, I had been tortured for a year, a fucking year. For a *broken nose*. They'd put a psychopath, totally unburdened by any guilt whatsoever for *matricide,* in the same cell as me!

Still, me and Ben were roommates, and, strange as it sounds, over the next two months, a friendship of sorts blossomed between us. I realized two things. The first was obvious from the start: he was a batshit crazy, homicidal, sociopathic, with zero empathy or remorse for what he had done. Second, though, was harder to stomach: as bad as he was, it was so nice to have a person to talk to, to play chess with, to help me up when I couldn't stand after a beating. Sure, we didn't have a real chessboard. We made a chess set using a sheet of notebook paper for the board and tore up another piece of paper for the pieces. All the while, Ben was a phenomenally nice guy, so much so that I would often forget that he'd murdered his mother.

Now that I had a roommate, I started to eat more. The guards still wouldn't feed me, but they did feed him, and out of a kindness and compassion that was totally out of line with the atrocity he'd committed, Ben always shared his food with me. They also left the water on once Ben was in the room, so I no longer had to drink out of a dirty toilet. Ben had been to prison previously, and we started to share our lives with one another.

One morning, on biscuits-and-gravy day, Ben started telling me about the best biscuits and gravy he had ever had, as he handed me one of the two biscuits from his breakfast tray. It was a true blessing.

"Bro," he said, "I had some biscuits as big as your head! Apalachee sucked, but they sure did feed you."

I laughed. "You're making that up."

"Naw, man, it's a psych camp. Everybody walks around like zombies. Everybody there is on medication. Thorazine. They call it the Thorazine shuffle. It's on a lake, so there are seagulls. Giant seagulls, biggest seagulls you've ever seen. Bigger than Yorkies and Pomeranians! The officers don't even search you coming out of the chow hall to see if you're stealing food because the seagulls are fearless, and if you come out with any food, the seagulls will attack you an' take it. The guards just watch to see who gets swarmed. Seagulls are drug addicts too, 'cause a lot of the inmates will pretend like they're taking their medication, then give it to the seagulls. The seagulls eat that shit up like candy. Have you ever seen a seagull tryin' to fly while high? That's the funniest thing you've ever seen, swerving and dipping and flapping in the air—they fly into each other and crash like something out of a cartoon!"

"Dude," I said, "I know you're making that up."

Ben looked at me, stared me straight in the eyes with that unearthly innocent face of his. "Josh, I'm telling you what I seen with my own eyes. If you get caught giving your medication to the seagulls, they'll throw you in confinement and add an additional charge to your record—animal abuse. Most of the people who are there have at least fifteen years—nut cases, so they don't care. One really funny thing, though: you never see any seagulls on chicken day or the day after. Really makes you wonder about that chicken they feed you."

Ben smiled with that devious smile. "Anyways," he went on, "ever since I killed my mom and my girlfriend, I've been wanting to try it again. What are they going to do to me? Give me another life sentence? Kill me? That's what they're already planning on doing anyway."

The mood was suddenly somber. We'd been sharing our space together for a couple of months already, and I *knew* Ben was a sociopath. But to hear him speak about murder out loud was still shocking. So many people talk about killing, but it's usually just bravado, for shock value. This was something else. Hearing somebody who had already killed two people, been caught and convicted of killing two people, casually talking about wanting to do it again was freaky.

All of a sudden, an epiphany hit me—*this was my way out!*

"I want you to kill me." I heard the words coming out of my mouth, simultaneously terrifying and liberating. "I will show you how to do a military-style blood choke so I don't suffer. You'll have to hold it for about thirty seconds. At three seconds, I'll pass out and lose consciousness. At seven seconds, my brain will start shutting down my organs. By eleven seconds, my brain should be suffering catastrophic failure and begin hemorrhaging, and by twenty seconds I should be long dead."

Did I really just say that out loud?

The look on Ben's face, so eager and excited, was terrifying.

"You are going to let me kill you?" Ben asked. The eager look on his face was like the look on the starving kid's face in the original Willy Wonka, when he sees all the free candy.

I nodded my head slightly.

Ben's eyes widened. "Let's do it! I am ready!"

I notice a bulge in his pants and realized that the thought of killing had excited him so much he'd become sexually aroused. He literally had a hard on for me. Well, for killing me.

As he started moving toward me prepared to choke me, I put my arm out to stop him.

"I need to write some things down first so that my family will know the truth about a few things, and so I can say goodbye."

I started writing letters to the people I was going to leave behind. I wrote two pages to Madeline, apologizing for all of my inadequacies and anything I'd ever done to hurt her. I told her that I forgave her for cheating on me, for Adam, told her that I still loved her, always would. I wrote a letter to my mother and three sisters, told my mother that I loved her and I forgave her for neglecting me and abusing me as a child. I told my mother that I forgave her for allowing my sisters to abuse me and molest me. I apologized for never having been good enough, for not giving her a grandchild, for not being perfect. I told my sisters that I was sorry for not being a better big brother, for having left at age fourteen to go live on my own instead of being there to protect them. I wrote a letter to my business partner, Buck, told him about how much of a privilege it was to teach alongside him, to have helped grow Revolutionary Martial Arts and Fitness. I told him that it was an honor to have called him my friend and to have had an opportunity to hear him share his wisdom with me.

I also wrote a letter to agent Derek Wallace, enumerating the incidents of professional misconduct and criminal behaviors he used in order to get me arrested and charged. I called him out for pretending to be a Pasco County Sheriffs officer, for pretending to be a member of the SWAT team investigating human trafficking. I called him out for using his position as an officer in the Florida Army Reserves to get Master Buck and me into his military police unit. I told him that entrapment was unethical and that if he had wanted to get back at me for having fucked his wife, he should've just punched me in the face like a normal person instead of following me around for two years. Last but not least, I told him that my death, my blood, was on his hands.

Finally, I wrote the hardest of the letters.

Dear Dad,

I'm sorry for how much this is going to hurt you. I'm also not sorry for how much this is going to hurt you. I have loved you more than any other person alive, my entire life. I have devot-

ed my entire life to earning your approval and earning your love. Never once have I heard you say, 'Josh, I'm proud of you.' For almost a year now I have been beaten unconscious three times per day, starved, pepper sprayed for the entertainment of the guards. For almost a year now, I have been denied medical attention, dehumanized and degraded, forced to kiss and lick the boots of the guards, forced to drink my own sewage from the toilet, literally forced to eat shit—fecal matter—for the entertainment of the guards. I have written you hundreds of letters, yet you have not once sent me a response. I have cried out for you every day, yet not once have you answered me. You were supposed to protect me as a child, but you weren't there. You turned a blind eye to all of the horrible things that Mom and my sisters did to me. You never intervened, never protected me. All the times I've told you what's going on, you've never believed me. As a child, you always told me to stop exaggerating and stop lying. but I'm not lying. I'm not exaggerating. I'm saying goodbye. Hopefully, you'll believe me now.

As I sealed this last letter, I turned to Ben and said, "Are you really ready to do this?"

With unbridled excitement, Ben affirmed. The guards counted us every half hour, so we waited until the next count, and as soon as it finished, Ben sat on my bunk, with me sitting directly in front of him. I leaned back and helped guide his arms to the perfect position to maximize the restriction of blood flow to my brain. I relaxed every muscle in my body, willed myself to pass out and die faster. Ben started squeezing, applying to tremendous pressure. In less than three seconds, everything went black.

And then—

An eternity went by.

Yet I was not alone.

I was floating in darkness, weightless. I was not scared, somehow. I knew that I was safe.

There was no pain. Just a sensation of nothing and everything. And it was so peaceful, just floating in the darkness. I was at peace, comfortable, content to just...exist.

I didn't know where I was, didn't matter. I felt...something like a pressure, but it was not unpleasant, more like a gentle embrace from a parent or a loved one, reassuring, calming, safe. I don't know how long I was there, but it felt like forever. Months, years, centuries. Time was meaningless. I heard a song by Stone Sour about not knowing how much time had passed and about how eternity felt like home. An overwhelming sensation of reassurance came over me. Everything was OK. Everything would be OK. I could stay there forever....

And I knew that I wanted to.

And then—

A different feeling, as though I was suddenly being pulled from a great distance, but no! I didn't want to go! The peace and the comfort was receding! No! I didn't want to leave!

Please!

I begged God to let me stay! Pain erupted somewhere. I didn't know quite where, because I didn't have a body, but it was overwhelming. Pressure, oh God, *the pressure!* Something was crushing me—and that horrible pain, I realized, was my lower back. The incredible pressure was my chest. I couldn't breathe. All at once, everything exploded with flashes of painful and piercing bright light. My head pounded is if somebody was hitting me with a sledgehammer over and over again, and I was shaking—but why? I could feel my arms and legs twitching and spasming uncontrollably, but they wouldn't respond to me. The pain just kept building and building. I couldn't breathe!

Why couldn't I breathe!

"Sounds like someone's having a seizure."

I could hear a shout as though from a great distance, then realized it was a prisoner in another cell. I opened my eyes to an assault of blinding light, felt my body. The upper part was on the bunk, but I was laying on my back. My hips were hanging off of the edge, and my legs were on the floor twitching. That explained the pain in my lower back. I tried to sit up, but my body wouldn't respond. My arms and legs were still twitching, and I realized I was having a severe seizure. I tried to speak, but there was no air in my lungs. I gasped for breath, started coughing. Pink froth erupted from my mouth. My arms and legs eventually stopped twitching as Ben helped me sit up.

"What the fuck, man? I told you not to let go for at least thirty seconds!" I said.

"Josh, I didn't let go for almost five minutes. And then I let go only because the rookie guard made an unexpected round. You laid there dead for over two minutes before having a seizure and coming back. I thought you were gone! Do you want me to try again now?"

Every inch of my body hurt. Throat, neck, pounding head— still gasping for breath.

"No," I said. "Gimme a few days to recover before we try that again."

TIGHTEN UP

Everything I had endured at the jail was horrific, and yet it was possible for things to be worse. I could not see it at the time, but from the perspective of being exposed to violence and degenerate behaviors, it could absolutely get worse. In jail, the system and facility has to keep you alive and mostly whole because not everyone who gets arrested is guilty, and if the guards allow horrible things to happen to everyone, they would get sued often by all the people who have their charges dropped, dismissed, or are found not guilty.

This does not hold true once you get sent to prison, as everyone in prison has been convicted, either by pleading guilty because of prosecutor and police intimidation or by being found guilty at trial.

There is no longer a significant risk of an innocent person getting released and bringing attention to the atrocities that they experienced.

Although I had pled guilty to the federal conspiracy charge and should have gone to a federal minimum security prison for a few months, the altercation with the correctional officer brought me into the state system. The year of torture I endured and the time spent trying to avoid a thirty-year sentence for breaking the guards nose had seen nearly the entire federal sentence completed. As such, off to the Florida Department of Corrections reception center I went.

I was picked up by the Florida Department of Corrections transport. Before they load you into a steel dog kennel inside the back of a van that looks normal from the outside, they shackle your feet and cuff your hands, then place a chain around your waist and lock your hands to your belly button area. As if that were not enough, though, they then connect a chain from your hands to your feet, and the final step is to place a military-grade plastic box around the cuffs and locks to prevent any movement of the cuffs or your hands. This device was supposedly invented by a former inmate who had escaped his cuffs more than once.

Shoved into a steel dog kennel with fifteen other full-size grown men, we spent nearly eight hours driving without food, water, or access to a bathroom, only to arrive at the Lake Butler Medical and Reception center for processing—a humiliating and dehumanizing process of stripping naked, freezing group showers, cavity searches, having your heads forcibly shaved, being screamed at like a recruit in Marine Corps boot camp, having any personal possessions such as letters or photos destroyed in front of you, watching inmates there be allowed to take anything they wanted for themselves, and then thrown into a box for a few weeks while they processed where to send you.

This whole experience is such a traumatic blur that lasted a few weeks that the only thing that stands out to me was seeing a young man stabbed in the throat with a pen because he hadn't paid a debt, and seeing a navy veteran beat to death—murdered—by the guards, for politely asking them not to call him a "nigger."

After the few weeks of processing, the transport process was repeated. The Florida Department of Corrections divided the state of Florida into three regions—north, central, and south. South Florida is where they housed those inmates they did not hate as much: low-security short-timers with nonviolent charges and those who had been model inmates for years. Central Florida was a mix of the more dangerous and less dangerous, longer sentences and shorter. But north Florida, that was where they sent the troublemakers, the inmates they wanted to disappear and be forgotten by the world. This was where they sent the cop killers, the serial killers, the worst of the rapists, and the inmates who had been violent problems. This was where they sent the mentally ill and those with large amounts of time, in the hopes that the inmates would be their own form of population control and kill each other.

Guess where they sent me.

This time, it was a much longer journey to the farthest corner of Florida: Century. Century is in the Florida Panhandle, a stone's throw away from Alabama. I believe that I was one of the rare exceptions at Century, as generally everyone sent to Century had fifteen or more years to serve. While the transportation process was the same, only longer, and the intake process just as demeaning and dehumanizing, it was not long before I found myself in the work camp that was just outside of the main prison complex at Century. The work camps were where the less dangerous and more mentally stable inmates were sent at most facilities, because they can reasonably be expected to stay in line and perform slave labor. I was quickly assigned to work in the kitchen because I was classified as too dangerous to be allowed any other work assignment that might take me outside of the compound.

It took less than three days for me to learn that this was a completely different culture, language, and social structure than anything I had ever experienced, seen on TV, or read about.

As I was untying my shoes at 8:30 a.m. after finishing my morning shift in the kitchens, a young, slender black kid walked past me and tapped me twice on the side of the knee with the back of his hand,

"Tighten up," was all he said as he kept walking. I had no clue what he meant by that, so I dismissed it without a second thought and continued untying my shoes.

My bunkmate Corey leaned down from the top bunk and asked me, "You gonna go tighten up? Dude is waiting to fight you."

The question caught me by surprise.

"What do you mean, fight me?" I said. "Why would I wanna fight him? I don't even know him."

With a small grin on his face, Corey said, "Bro, I'm gonna start calling you *Chili Soup*, 'cause you are square and green as fuck, just like them chili-flavored ramen noodles. He's calling you out to fight. If you don't go fight him, everyone is going to know that you are a soft bitch, and you're gonna have a lot of problems with people taking advantage of you."

"Well, damn," I said, "then I guess I don't have a choice."

As I was retying my shoes, Corey said to me, "Be careful, Josh. He's a *swift* fighter. He learned that shit in juvie, and he's been knockin' bitches out at least once a week for months."

In nearly twenty-five years of martial arts experience, I'd never heard of a style of fighting called *swift* so I completely dismissed everything Corey said and proceeded to follow the young kid to a corner of the dormitory called the Grid because it was a blind spot from the officer's station's field of vision, so all the nonspontaneous fights happened here. The area that we would be fighting was approximately three feet wide by six feet long, with stainless steel bunk beds on either side. Not a lot of room to maneuver, with a lot of sharp edges that could be incredibly dangerous in the heat of a fight should I make a mistake.

"Catch the wall," he said, like it was a position of disadvantage. *Catch the wall? Absolutely!* I was no fool, and the last thing I wanted was to have my back toward his friends while I was fighting him.

I placed my back against the wall and then took one step forward. I assumed the fighting stance that the Marine Corps likes to call basic warrior position, relaxed, evenly balanced, with 50 percent of your weight on your front leg and 50 percent of your weight on your back leg, directly facing your opponent, shoulders rolled slightly forward so that the sensitive areas of your ribs and stomach are somewhat protected, first knuckle of your hands touching the bottom orbit of your eye, hands in loose fists and elbows hanging naturally, completely relaxed. This position protects your face, head, neck, torso, and genitals, while allowing you a clear field of vision and a balanced position so that you can move or strike quickly, forward or backward, with either hand or leg. There's no jumping around like Bruce Lee, no wasted energy.

The kid squared up with me and started bouncing a little as if he thought he was a boxer. I remained motionless in the basic warrior position. He bobbed and weaved, moving forward and back, side to side. It was an absolute waste of energy. Plus, it made him like an ugly peacock with bad teeth trying to scare me and impress everyone else.

I threw a jab with my left, not intending to hit him, but merely to gauge his reflexes and his style. He pranced out of the way, and he *was* fast, no denying. I threw a quick kick with my front leg to see if he was quick on his feet too. It didn't land, nor was it intended to, but he started laughing, this peacock-looking kid, thinking I was slow and clumsy.

I am right-handed and right-side dominant. My right hand and right leg were slightly offset to the rear of my left hand and left foot.

Since this kid knew he was fast and thought I was some big, slow, white boy, I let my hands drop a little bit to the center of my chest hoping that he would try to punch me in the now-exposed left side of my face.

My wish was granted—he took a swing for the left side of my jaw, but I was already moving forward into the punch while turning my face and body to avoid the hit. That right hand that he thought I dropped was strategically poised to drive my elbow into the side of his neck, and just as his punch narrowly missed my face, every ounce of my 240-pound frame drove my elbow right into his throat.

Now, I have seen enough movies that portrayed the dangers of prison, to know there was only one way this could go: I had to kill this motherfucker. The question was how. Maybe I'd break his spine when the time came, but in that moment, pain was exploding through my neck and right shoulder. I'd hit him so hard that I almost dislocated my own shoulder. His legs immediately buckled and started twitching as he collapsed to the floor. I stepped back while he lay there—I could smell that he had voided his bowels. Because of where my punch landed, he could still breathe and speak, no problem—but he'd lost the use of most of his body. As he continued struggling to stand, his legs just keep twitching, sliding and moving in unnatural ways.

Suddenly, he said to me, "Go sit down. You don't want to fight."

* * *

Throughout my life, I have been taught to see things through to completion. Anything worth doing is worth doing correctly. Doing something half-assed only resulted in consequences, wasted energy, and having to do it over and over until it was done.

When I was about twelve or thirteen years old, after I had moved in with my father, we had a comfortable division of labor in the home. Whoever cooked was exempt from cleanup. My father and I took turns cooking and, likewise, took turns cleaning up. One particular evening, I started doing the dishes after he'd cooked. I really wanted to watch the newest episode of *Stargate SG-1* that was coming out that evening, so I hurried through washing the dishes. When I was finished, dad inspected the dishes.

"Nope," he said as he examined the first pan, placing it back in the sink. "Also nope. Josh, you need to wash all of these over again. They are not clean. There is still grease on them."

Begrudgingly, I rewashed everything. What originally had taken me about twenty minutes had now consumed an hour of my evening. *Stargate* was coming on in a few minutes.

"Dad," I said as I dried my hands. "They're clean now."

Dad came in and inspected the dishes. This time, he pulled about half of them out and told me to rewash them because they were still dirty.

By the time they were all clean, what should have taken me thirty minutes had taken me three hours because I kept doing a half-assed job. More importantly, I had missed *Stargate*. (This was before Netflix and DVR. Missing the episode meant I would have to wait until it came out on DVD and buy the entire set.). I was very upset. Dad watched *Stargate* while I washed dishes. The lesson here was to do it right the first time, see it through to full completion, or pay the price.

* * *

In that moment when I was presented with an easy way out of the conflict, this lesson from my father was front and center in my mind.

If I accepted the easy way out now, how many more times would I be forced to fight that could be avoided if I saw this through to the fullest completion? What consequences would I have to endure if I took this shortcut instead of doing it right the first time? The stakes were clearly higher than missing an episode of a TV show. I did not want to continue fighting any more than I wanted to continue washing the dishes that night with my dad.

"You're right," I replied. "I never did want to fight. But here we are, and now the fight doesn't end until I've had enough. Stand your ass up and fight!"

All at once, seven other black men in the dormitory all stood up. One told me, "We is gonna take this fade for him."

I had no idea what that meant, but I quickly learned that the kid who had just shit his pants was a gang member, and all seven of his comrades were stepping in to fight on his behalf. I later learned what should have been obvious but wasn't to a nice Jewish guy like me from the suburbs: *most* gangs have some variation of a rule where nobody outside the gang can be allowed to get away with beating their member in a fight. The moment the peacock's knees hit the ground, the Magnificent 7 were duty-bound to get in and beat the crap out of me. First, because I was a nongang member, but second, because running my mouth guaranteed that they all *had* to teach me a lesson.

If you have ever seen a Jason Statham *Transporter* movie or a Matt Damon Jason Bourne movie, you can envision the fight that ensued.

I was standing in that space between two bunks, three feet wide, as seven men approached with the intention of breaking every bone in my body. Maybe they appeared more wolflike or predatory in memory than they were in reality, but in the moment, I was like baby Simba from the Lion King with all of the hyenas coming at me, menacing.

I took one step backward, knowing that the space was narrow enough to ensure they could only approach me one or two at a time—my only chance of survival. The first two to get close were both about five nine and two hundred pounds apiece, athletically built like wrestlers. As the first threw a punch at my face, I weaved to my left and caught his wrist in my right hand while slamming my left forearm just behind the elbow joint on his arm. I can't even describe to you the sickening sound that his arm made as it broke, but he screamed in agony as I continued the clockwise motion, bringing his face forcefully into the steel support beam of the bunk bed, suddenly cutting his scream short as I rendered him unconscious from the blunt trauma to the head.

As he collapsed, his friend attempted to grab me by the front of my shirt using both hands. He succeeded in grabbing the front of my shirt, but I was already turning counterclockwise, bringing my right arm over his arms while trapping his wrists and hands against my chest, causing his arms to cross in a very unflattering way. I continued my counterclockwise motion, drawing him forward and down as he twisted from the crossed arms. Using his momentum in that situation, I caused him to trip over the unconscious form of his buddy, and as he went down, I stomped on the side of his face with my heel. The Marine Corps calls this the "All-American curb stomp," but whatever you call it, it resulted in a crunch as his jaw broke and five teeth came out of his mouth.

I turned around just in time to block a punch from the third guy with both of my forearms, and then I managed to get out of the way of his second punch by lunging forward into his attack with my left arm outside of his right arm and my right arm close to his torso as if I was reaching over his shoulder. I moved into the punch, trapping his right arm over my right shoulder with my right forearm against the side of his neck and my left hand on the back of his shoulder. Yanking down hard as I took a step back, I cracked his jaw against the steel edge of the bunk bed and then drove my knee into his sternum three times before taking two steps backward toward the wall as I drove his face into the floor with his arm up behind his back.

I slammed my knee into his elbow while yanking on his wrist with all of my might, and again came that indescribable, sickening crunch as his arm bent in a direction that nature had not intended. I think he was already unconscious from hitting the floor with his face since I didn't hear any screams. As I got up to meet the fourth guy, I was not quite fast enough, and his overlong thumbnail caught my upper lip, splitting it wide open. His punch missed, but the nail did some serious damage. This guy was more aggressive than the other four I had fought thus far, and I was a little bit surprised by his intensity.

I spent a good four or five seconds just blocking all of his punches with my forearms and my hands. If you've never been in a real fight, you know that five seconds might as well be five years. I finally saw an opening and kicked just below the front of his kneecap like I was kicking a soccer ball with the instep of my foot. This caused his leg to snap back and his head to snap down, right into my open-handed palm strike to his face. As his head snapped up, I reach around with my other hand and grabbed the back of his head to crank his head around. My intention was to break his neck, but fortunately for him and for me, his buddy, guy number five, was trying to punch me with a haymaker. I cranked his head around and moved it into the path of the haymaker, so his buddy knocked him out for me.

Guy number five paused for a moment, stunned and confused that he had just knocked out his friend instead of me. I used that moment to kick him in the chin with a front-snap kick, and he went tumbling over a nearby bed.

Number six tried to hit me, but the positioning was perfect for me, and I stepped in and hit him dead center in his throat. He collapsed to the ground, choking and coughing but very much alive.

Now I know what you're thinking: there's no way this action-movie story could be true. It's too Hollywood perfect. Right? Well, I can assure you the story is 100 percent true, and it doesn't have the happy ending that Hollywood would require. Gang member number seven had not yet had his go.

Gang member number seven charged me, 220 pounds of solid muscle, ten years of pent-up prison rage, and a lifetime of hatred toward white people. He rained down blow after blow, and while I blocked all of his swings, he very quickly pushed me backward into the small space between the bunks where I tripped over one of the first gang members and fell backward into a sitting position as he continued to rain down on me. I stayed in that fetal position, as he just punched the forearms covering my face—five, ten, fifteen times or more. Truth be told, I stopped counting, and eventually, thank the Lord, he stopped punching. Not once did he land a blow to my face or body, but for the next two weeks, my forearms were blacker than he was.

After he backed off, I got up slow and realized my face was bleeding profusely from the split lip. No doubt, I needed stitches. But how could I get stitches without telling the guards what had just happened?

Suddenly, the loudspeakers blasted. "Count time! Count time! Everybody get ready for count! On your bunks!"

Now the guards were about to come in. I was fucked. I started to walk over to my bunk and looked down at one of the gang members who had jumped me as he was trying to get up, and I deliberately stepped on his hand and ground my heels into his fingers as I passed by. Then I glanced around and noticed that some of the other guys in the dorm were helping the injured get up and get to their bunks so the guards would remain unaware. Heat on one of us was bad for all of us.

I placed my chin in my hands while sitting on my bunk, so that my face remained covered and the guards couldn't see any of the blood or injuries. An officer came in and walked up and down the rows of the bunks to count the inmates. There were seventy-six of us, all sitting upright in neatly organized rows on numbered bunks. Sadly, the only two requirements to be a prison guard in Florida were (1) no felony convictions and (2) over the age of eighteen—no need to even have a high school diploma or GED. If you could count to seventy-five, you were golden.

The officer counted us up, then conferred with a second officer who walked in. The second officer recounted, then conferenced with the first officer. They both looked confused. I knew they were going to count us again. I could feel the hot, wet blood trickling down my chin and onto my hands, and I started sweating. If this took much longer, I was gonna have some explaining to do. The officers went up and down the rows frantically counting us again, and this time when they conferred with each other I could see visible relief on each of their faces. As soon as they left, I grabbed a towel off of my bunk and held it to my face where I was bleeding.

"Holy fucking shit, nigga! I didn't know you could fight like that! That was like some super, secret agent, *Matrix*, Steven Segal shit! You are like Bruce Lee, bro!" Corey leaned forward off of the bunk above me looking at me in awe.

"No man," I said, "I lost. I was curled up in a ball trying to protect my face. And my arms freaking hurt like somebody hit me with a baseball bat."

"The fuck you mean? Bro, are you fucking high? You just fought eight gang members, only one of them walked away without assistance, and all you have is a little scratch on your face? You kicked their fucking asses! I could hear the bones break from across the dorm! Teeth flying ten feet! You knocked one asshole out using the other asshole's fist. You ripped someone's arm out of his shoulder while you kicked a bitch in the face! Bro that's the nastiest shit I've ever seen in my entire life, and I've seen some shit, man!"

"Yard open! Yard open! Everybody outside for rec!" the announcement came over the loudspeaker.

All of the doors buzzed, and everybody got up to go outside. This was exactly the opportunity that I needed. I shuffled out the door with everyone else and casually wandered around the yard for about five minutes. Roughly, three hundred people were milling with the basketball courts kicked into full swing. This was all the excuse I needed in order to get medical attention without admitting wrongdoing. I've seen enough movies to know what happens if you snitch. I made my way to the basketball court and stood on the sidelines with my hand covering my face for a few minutes. When one of the guys got the basketball, I acted like I was gonna snatch it out of his hand and then threw myself backward onto the ground as if I had caught an elbow to the face. Now I had an excuse as to why my lip was split. I got up, blood dripping all over my face and my hands, and walked to the nearest guard.

"Excuse me, sir. I need to go to medical. I think I need stitches."

Of course, the officer tried to ignore me, and I repeated myself now that I was closer to him. As he glanced over at me nonchalantly, his eyes widened when he saw all the blood.

"What the fuck happened to you, inmate?" he said.

"Didn't you just see me catch an elbow to the face on the basketball court?" I replied. "Can I please go to medical?"

I tried my very best to hide the sarcasm in my voice, because I knew this inbred officer in the panhandle of Florida was dumber than corn. I'd made sure that my fall happened directly in front of him, made sure that he was a witness to my lip being split in a nonaggressive, nonfight situation. He looked me up and down a few more times and then told me to go with him to speak to the captain. I knew it took him some serious mental energy for him to process what was going on while struggling to chew on the piece of straw in this mouth, but this was progress.

We walked about two hundred feet across the compound to the captain's office and then, after knocking on the door and telling the captain he needed to deal with me, the officer left to go back to his hay-chewing duties.

The captain, an older black man, looked me up and down and then said, "Who were you fighting with?"

OK, I thought, *here goes. Let's see how good my poker game is.*

"Fighting? I just caught an elbow on the basketball court." I tried to look as innocent and dumbfounded as possible.

"Son, I know you were fighting because I've never seen you on a basketball court in my life. Now don't worry. I won't let anybody hurt you for telling me the truth. Who did this to you?"

Think fast, Josh. Think fast. "Sir, I've only been on the compound for a couple of days. I'm new here. I'm not afraid of anybody here, and I don't think I have any reason to be. I'm not gonna tell you that somebody did this to me when nobody did. Can't I please get some medical attention? I'm bleeding all over your floor."

He leaned forward across his desk, either attempting to look intimidating or to look like he cared, like I could trust him. Either way, he failed. Sensing my skepticism, he said, "This is your last chance, inmate. Tell me who did this to you, and I'll get them off the compound so you will be safe. I cannot protect you if you don't tell me what happened."

"Just…basketball. I ran into another player's elbow. It was an accident, and I think I might need stitches."

Now the captain shot me a curious look. "Do you understand, inmate, that if you change your story later, I'm going to throw you in solitary confinement for lying to an officer?"

Of course, I understood all too well. But if I wasn't willing to snitch then, snitching later would be even worse—all sides would punish me for telling the truth. As I nodded my understanding, I was directed to pass through a closed doorway into an adjacent room where a certified nursing assistant was waiting. She was neither qualified nor comfortable doing stitches on my face. As she gave me butterfly strips to pull my lip back together, she said that this was the best I was going to get. I took the butterfly strips from her and did the best I could to finish the job. I knew it was going to leave a scar because I had no idea what I was doing. When I finished, I left the clinic and walked back to my dormitory.

Upon reentering my dorm, the young black kid who'd asked me to tighten up walked up to me and said, "We good?"

"Yeah, man, we're good."

He nodded his head and walked off, like that was the end of it. He got about ten feet away and then glanced over his shoulder and said, "By the way, my name is Gator. You fight pretty good, for a white boy." And that was the end of that.

There's a line made famous by the Matrix movies with Keanu Reeves. The second movie, I think. "You never truly know someone until you have fought them."

For most of my life, that was one of the singularly most profound ideas I had ever encountered. I assume that you are not a fighter, but I can tell you that for someone who is a real fighter, a warrior, when you are engaged in a real fight (rather than friendly sparring in a gym), everything else fades away as the adrenaline pumps through your veins. In that moment, there's a very cliché Hollywood-esque tunnel vision, where all of the colors, the sounds, the smells are a hundred times more vivid than what you normally perceive going through day-to-day life, but all of the surroundings disappear. Nothing else matters but the present moment.

Most fighters who make a career of fighting are no different than any other drug addict, because what happens to your senses and perceptions is very similar to an intense high. Your perception of time slows down, and your memories of the fight are particularly vivid, even if you do not recall everything that was going on around you. All of the writers who attempt to describe a fight but have never been in a fight fail to adequately encompass the vivid nature of a fight. I can tell when a fight is written in a story by somebody who's never been in a real fight.

It took me some time to realize certain things about prison culture, as it is difficult to be meditative or develop philosophical insights on a subject while you are drowning in it and learning to swim. But my arrival at Century Correctional Institution and the vortex of violence that so quickly sucked me in forced my eyes open on a few issues. For starters, I had never been in a real fight. Sure, I had fought in the gym and in the dojo. I had participated in come competitions and tournaments. I had broken up a few bar fights or scuffles over the years. But this was the first time that I had to fight for my life, where every fight was someone sincerely trying to hurt me with no rules and no one to save me, and this was the first time in my life where even looking at someone for a moment could be enough to be forced into fighting for my life.

For years, I had been telling myself and others that I wish I could have a real situation to test my skills that I had spent years honing. I had prayed for it. Now that I had it, I realized that I hated it. I didn't like the adrenaline dump. The racing heart. The fear. I also found that in the moment, when everything else faded away, I did not experience a rush of pleasure or enjoy hurting others. But I was quickly learning that having visible military tattoos, cauliflower ear, and having been in the newspaper for teaching martial arts made me a target. I would end up forced to fight more often than was normal even in prison, because the culture was such that they needed to test themselves against the military, against the expensive martial arts they see in the movies, and against the white man. I was to be a target because I was good at fighting. And I was to be a target if I won or a victim if I lost.

I did not want to spend my time fighting, and I attempted to embrace the idea that if I pushed the envelope to the extreme and made an example of those who I had to fight, I would maybe keep the fights to a minimum. If the reputation spread that picking a fight with me was likely to end up with someone going to the hospital seriously injured, I thought that maybe 90 percent of the potential fights could be avoided by those looking for an easy mark.

I have spent countless hours trying to understand why there was so much violence, why there was a culture where violence was not only expected but also your willingness to engage in it and your proficiency at it determined your worth as a man and your position in the social hierarchy. Everyone in academia or politics has different ideas, including that it is caused by the culture of abuse that slave owners perpetrated on generations of black men, or that the lack of education in poor communities caused it. I disagree. I have concluded that the answer is much more simple, as uncomfortable as it may be.

First, in a place where you have no control over anything and are generally powerless, physically dominating someone gives the perception of power or control. Outside of prison. this is usually more subtle and less physical, but in prison, you have no wealth, no assets, and the act of dominance is much more primitive. Humans have been seeking to control each other since the dawn of time.

Second, most people think that prison is a place of bustling activity, where everyone has a job and their minds are stimulated with opportunities to learn or better oneself. This could not be further from the truth. Most prisons have about fifteen hundred inmates, but less than three hundred of them have actual jobs or are able to participate in the limited programs for education or betterment. While everyone has a job assignment, the remaining twelve hundred men are usually assigned as "rec orderly," meaning that they sit on the rec yard and do nothing all day. The sheer boredom of being in a concrete box or an empty field twenty-four hours per day for years at a time leads to an incredible amount of frustration and pent-up tension. This needs an outlet, and violence is an explosive expression of that pent up boredom and rage being released.

And finally, I have concluded that the culture of violence is a drug addiction. In a place where you are so isolated and numb, to feel something, to feel anything, is an escape from the reality you are forced to live in. The incredible adrenaline rush that makes your heart race, brings all the colors and sounds into sharp and vivid focus, that is a high. The feeling after a fight is euphoric, after all the adrenaline fades leaving you with a sense of incredible peace and calm. And if you won, the feeling of being a celebrity for a few days is intoxicating.

In a place that is full of addicts, fighting is a drug, and the most accessible one.

MY NAME IS SIN

There was a sergeant at Century Correctional Facility's Forced Labor Camp, an old, heavyset homosexual known for preying on younger white inmates. It was bad enough that he'd already strip-searched me in the chapel five times in three days. Then he made me bend over at the waist while spreading my butt cheeks apart with my hands and pointed a flashlight into my asshole saying, "Woohoo, lookie here! Wonder how much we could fit in there!"

I had no recourse but to file a complaint, but it might not have been the smartest thing I've ever done. Next thing I knew, they were shipping me to Century Correctional Institution's main compound, one of the five most dangerous facilities in the entire state of Florida.

This was somehow safer for me than allowing me to remain at the work camp where I had filed a complaint against one of the officers for sexual assault.

The main area was one of the older compounds in the state of Florida, and at a glance, it had roughly the same layout as any other. After going through the normal process of being issued sheets and blankets and uniforms and then being directed to our respective dormitories, I made my way in. Within five minutes of entering the dorm, I was approached by a giant white guy with a shaved head, built like a bodybuilder, six foot three inches and 260 pounds of solid muscle. The guy was a human wall.

"Hey, man. Welcome to the dorm. I am Israel. You look like a stand-up guy, so if you need anything you come talk to me. And after chow tonight, you come talk to me at my bunk. I want to know where your head's at."

Then he turned to walk away, revealing an enormous swastika tattooed on his back.

I wasn't sure what he meant by "you look like a stand-up guy," but I had a feeling it was code for *white*.

As I got settled in, I got down to the most important order of business: threat assessment. Israel had already identified himself as a potential problem. Then there were five black guys huddled in the corner, behaving like they were trying to hide something. Something was getting passed between them and tucked away. Drugs were the best bet. Obviously, there's a thriving drug-and-tobacco black market in both jail and prison, usually brought in by the guards and not the visitors. As I continued to scope around, I saw another white guy with a shaved head doing tattoos on somebody laying on their belly on an empty bunk. Then there were a few guys interspersed reading books, Bibles, sleeping.

The dorm seemed quiet. I hoped it would remain this way. In fact, I'd heard from other inmates that the library was one of the best in the entire state. As soon as I got settled, I put in a request form to go to the library and get some books. As I turned around from the request box, I bumped into a black guy and accidentally made him spill his bowl of food.

"Oh man," I said, "my bad! I'm so sorry."

"*Oh hell naw!*" He was ready to throw hands. "Get in the Grid, cracka!"

Then the intercom blasted. "Count time! Count time! On your bunks! Count time!"

"You saved by the bell, white boy!" He sneered. "Soon as count clears, get in the Grid. I's gonna fuck you up!"

I went straight to my bunk. Count lasted an hour—the entire time, he sat on his bunk on the other side of the door, beating his chest and saying loudly for everyone to hear, "Fuck you up, bitch-ass cracker. Pussy-ass white boy. Fuck you up, bitch. Soon as count clears, get in the Grid, punk-ass white boy!"

I kept my mouth shut, but soon as count cleared, I hopped off of my bunk and walked over to the corner of the dorm known as the Grid. By the time I got there, he was already gone.

The old man sitting on the bunk closest to the Grid said to me, "He didn't want to fight you. He was selling *wolf tickets*."

"Wolf tickets?" I replied.

"Yeah, wolf tickets," the old man said. "He beats his chest and acts really tough for everyone to see, so they think he's a predator. He's counting on being so intimidating that you don't show up to fight. He looks like a bad ass. You look like a bitch. He gets street credit for being tough, without any risk. Eight out of ten times, it works. You're a young white boy, good-looking, well-spoken. According to prison rules, you're soft, you can't fight, and so you're an easy mark on his belt without actually having to do anything. The only problem for him is that you actually showed up. Everybody saw you show up, and he didn't. But don't worry about it. He's all talk."

As we all went to chow, I could see him in the line. He wouldn't make eye contact with me. That was fine by me. I wasn't looking for a fight.

When I got back to the dorm after chow, Israel waved me over to his bunk. Not looking to make any more enemies my first day here, I obliged him. Dreading what I was about to hear or be asked, I sat down on the footlocker next to his bed. He pulled out some handwritten papers and started talking to me about the supremacy of the white race and how we don't interact with the inferior, ignorant blacks. He told me how, clearly, I had courage and heart to go stand up and fight. He let me know he was a member of the Aryan Brotherhood.

"The Brotherhood doesn't really have much of a presence in Florida prisons, but we got an unofficial truce between us, the Pagans, and the Unforgiven in prisons."

He started showing me these crazy handwritten pamphlets, mission statements with ethos, codes of conduct, rules, and expectations, all written up in a military style like general orders. No surprise, Israel kept using the word *nigger* and the word *kike*. He saw my Marine Corps tattoos on my forearm, and tried to tell me how I should join his brotherhood, just like the brotherhood I had in the Marine Corps, with structure and discipline, honor and courage.

I have light hair and blue eyes, and I look like I could have descended from Vikings, but the fact is, I'm a born and raised Ashkenazi Jew, and my grandparents survived Auschwitz, Dachau, and Birkenau. I did not want any part of a neo-Nazi or white supremacist organization.

I politely told him I would consider his suggestion, but added that I wasn't making any commitments at this time. What the hell else was I supposed to do?

After a few weeks, I'd managed to spend enough time in the law library to file a Federal Section 1983 civil rights lawsuit against the jail where I had been beaten and tortured for a year. In those weeks, I had managed to avoid any altercations and had even hustled up enough cash gambling on chess games to pay the tattoo man for a tattoo! What prison sentence would be complete without a jailhouse tattoo, right?

But what to get?

I decided that I was going to get a tattoo of a scorecard of sorts, to keep score of every person whose life I had significantly altered by violence. This way, I could keep a log of what a badass I was, for all time.

I got a bottle cap from a Gatorade bottle, and I decided it was the perfect size. Each person who I had fought and severely injured was going to get a "dead" smiley face. Not very complicated, just a perfect circle with the letter X where each eye should be. And as an added bonus, a Gatorade bottle cap is pretty universal, so if I ever needed to add more faces to the tattoo, it would be easy enough to keep up the theme. As of this moment, there were twelve dead smiley faces to represent the twelve people I had severely injured who would never forget having fought me.

The tattoo man was another white supremacist who everyone called Stewie on account of the giant *Family Guy* tattoos all over his back and chest. I paid him two bags of coffee, approximately twelve dollars in actual cost but the equivalent of about $240 value in the free world.

For a point of reference, the minimum wage in Florida at the time was about eight dollars per hour. The average wage for inmates was zero dollars per hour, and those rare and highly coveted paid positions started around ten cents an hour and maxed out after years of experience at less than a dollar. Even if your family put a million dollars in your canteen account, you were limited to a hundred dollars per week that you could spend. Currency was measured with food, ramen soups being the most common, like a twenty-dollar bill, and coffee being the highest form of currency as one six-dollar bag cost more than anyone but the highest paid inmates made in a week. A rough currency exchange would put the street value of a transaction in prison at twenty time higher than the actual dollar amount. When the dormitory cleared out, I laid down on the empty bunk, and Stewie took a piece of paper that he had sketched the tattoo on and pressed it against my side. He used some kind of pen ink to leave the design on the side of my ribs, then he started tattooing.

You might be wondering how he managed to get a tattoo gun, needles, and ink into a prison unnoticed. Let me tell you: he didn't. The needles were either actual staples or springs from pens stolen from the guard stations. The tattoo gun was cobbled together by using the motor from an electric shaver or from an electric pencil sharpener stolen from the law library or the education center. And, finally, we created our own ink by taking hair grease and toilet paper sold at the canteen, rolled up into a wick, set inside of a steel locker, then set on fire so that the soot collected on the lid of the locker. Mix that soot with instant coffee and, voila, you've got tattoo ink. Genius, right? Alas, probably not FDA approved.

Now, tattoos hurt. We all know this. Generally, when you get a tattoo, the tattoo artist uses an assembly that is a cluster of needles set in a tight circle or a cluster of needles set in a line like a paint brush. Not so in prison. In prison, you only have a single needle, and with a single needle, you have to go over the same area, over and over again. Each time, it hurts more than the last as the area is already bleeding and irritated. And on your rib cage? A tattoo will hurt even under the best of circumstances.

"Hey, Stewie," I said, vibrating with pain, "I need to get ahold of my dad and let him know I'm alive and safe, maybe get some money on my canteen account. You know anyone who will let me get on the phone?"

Stewie paused for a moment, as if deciding whether I could be trusted or not, then said, "If you want to get on the phone, you need to talk to one of the gangs because they control the phones. You're white, so you probably won't have any luck with the niggers. Talk to Sin."

"Sin?" I asked.

"If you don't know Sin, you are shit out of luck," Stewie said. "You'll find out who he is when he wants you to know who he is. Till then, you can take your chances with the dirty niggers or get on the regular prison phone with the rest of us."

The tattoo was supposed to be rows of four, going down my side like a scoreboard. They were all supposed to be identical, each face a perfect circle, with a straight line for the mouth and *X*'s for eyes, dead eyes. Stewie took it upon himself to make them alternate, smile, straight, smile, straight.

"What the fuck, man!" I said. "That isn't what I paid for!"

"Artistic liberty," he said. "I'll give you a discount if you're that unhappy about it."

"Hell yeah, I'm unhappy!" I replied. "It isn't like I can erase it! Fuck!"

Exasperated, I stormed off to my bunk.

One of the things that really surprised me about prison was the number of cell phones and the amount of drugs that could be found. In any given dorm, there are usually one to three cell phones, and enough drugs for *everyone* to partake. You realize very quickly who is participating in nefarious or illicit activity, because anytime an officer is approaching the dorm from the outside at least one inmate shouts, "Cheeseburger!" or, "One time!" At least, that's what they said here. It varies compound to compound, but there's always some kind of warning that guards are coming, something seemingly innocuous that also displays the level of ignorance and stupidity of the inmates. There were no cheeseburgers in prison, just like there were no dairy products, and no real beef. Why would anyone think that screaming, "Cheeseburger!" would be inconspicuous? Just because the majority of the officers were inbred country trash of all races, most with no education past high school and some even less, it didn't follow that they couldn't tell a warning from a holler.

Just as soon as someone shouted, "Cheeseburger!" there'd be a flurry of activity from the corner of the dorm where guys had been smoking some foul-smelling substance they called K2. I think it was the synthetic weed that gas stations sold, sometimes called "incense," which is really just grass or tobacco that's been sprayed with roach killer. Once, a scramble of activity erupted about twenty feet away from me where a skinny white guy with lots of tattoos and glasses was sitting on his bunk reading. Someone ran from him to the toilet area clutching something black in his hand.

"Everyone, on your bunks!" the officer shouted as he walked into the dorm. There were three other officers with him. They made a beeline for the skinny white guy with the glasses.

"Stand up, inmate!" the officer ordered. "Unlock your locker and step away from the bunk."

The young man complied, saying nothing. He had a smile on his face, a smug grin. The officers dumped his belongings on the floor, yanking the blanket and sheets off his mattress, pulling out a pocket knife to cut open his pillow and his mattress to search the insides. They tore apart his Bible and dumped his shampoo on the photographs of his family.

"Sarge," the inmate said, "the shampoo is clear. Can you please stop the officers from dumping it on my photos? If there was anything hidden in the shampoo, they'd be able to see it without pouring it all out and destroying my pictures."

"Silence, inmate!" The sergeant sneered. "I know you have a phone. I am going to find it, and if I don't, I will be back to plant one on you."

"I don't know what you're talking about," the young man said. "I've been sitting here minding my own business for hours, reading a book."

Frustrated by the lack of drama and by the lack of contraband, the officers turned to the surrounding inmates and shook down their bunks and their lockers as well. All in all, they tore apart six bunks, six mattresses, six pillows, and dumped all of the belongings of six inmates in one large pile that was now covered in soap and shampoo.

"Enough!" the sergeant said. "Let's go."

The officers left the dorm as five of the six inmates who had just had their lives turned upside down started putting their belongings and beds back together. The young man who was the target of their wrath and hostility walked across the dorm to Stewie. I couldn't hear what they were talking about, but I could see visible relief on the young man's face as they chatted.

I waited for things to die down and for the affected inmates to finish putting their areas back together. After about an hour, curiosity got the better of me. I approached the young man and struck up a conversation.

"Hey, what was that all about?" I asked him. "You keep to yourself and mind your own business. Why were the officers on you like that?"

"I don't know. I think it's because they don't like my tattoos."

He was covered in tattoos. I glanced up and down quickly, briefly checking them out. There was nothing spectacular to see. In fact, the tattoos weren't even very good. Nothing jumped out at me as inappropriate or any cause for hostility. There were no swastikas, no nudity, no violence. He had got some girls' names, some random pictures and tribal symbols, and one tattoo of a fish.

"There's nothing wrong with your tattoos, man," I said. "That doesn't make any sense. Anyways, I'm Josh. I've got some good books if you need one."

"I don't normally talk to people I don't know," he said, "especially new people. But you seem innocent enough and intelligent. My name's Sin."

I did a double take. *This* was the famous Sin?

"Good to meet you, Sin," I said. "You play chess?"

"No, man. It's not really my game. I never learned how to play. Anyway, I got some things I have to take care of. Talk to you later."

Watching him walk away, I couldn't believe it. I'd assumed Sin was a person of serious authority, somebody tough and dominant. This guy couldn't be the same person—this scrawny, dark-haired, Chicken Little–looking dude with glasses and tattoos, soft spoken, humble, and totally reserved.

I wanted to hear more about him, wanted to know more. Good thing I had books and I could sit on my bunk, pretending to read while closely observing. I had a direct line of sight from my bunk to his. I was determined to understand who this guy was and what was going on.

Over the course of a week, I diligently observed the comings and goings of Sin and of the people who regularly interacted with him. He and Stewie had frequent, almost-daily interactions, and I saw him paying Stewie every time he came back from the canteen line. He never got any tattoos from Stewie, and Stewie didn't do any special particular thing for him as far as I could tell. Far as I could see, Sin didn't do any drugs, although he would smoke the occasional cigarette, and he didn't get into confrontations or fights. He always had money, always had a locker full of snacks, and he had frequent visitors from our dorm and others who seemed to sneak in from other dorms around the compound. Sometimes, those visitors would sit on the floor next to his bunk and rest their head against his hip or his shoulder.

At first I thought he was gay, but there were too many different people who came over and spent time sitting in such close proximity

to him, but never exactly interacting with him. And it was strange—
he was always reading his book when they were there, yet I was pretty
sure that he didn't actually read very much, because he never seemed
to get any farther in his book. I didn't see him turning any pages—he
just kept the thing on his knees, held with both hands at the bottom
center.

Slowly, it dawned on me: he was texting or surfing the internet
on a cell phone and using the book as cover.

That explained why he always had visitors, why they always
brought him coffee and snacks and other forms of prison currency.

They were *paying him to send text messages* or to look things up
on the internet!

One thing that had always truly baffled me: Every time somebody new came into the dorm, the whole group of existing prisoners
would already immediately know what the new person's charges were,
what they were in prison for, and all their personal information. But
now I got it—Sin had the 411.

But if he always had a phone on him, how did the officers not
find it?

Making the educated guess that he was always packing a phone,
I decided I was going to take the initiative to see if he'd let me use
that phone. I knew I'd look like a real ass if I was wrong, but I had
to make a move. I wrote my mom's cell phone number and my dad's
cell phone number on a little piece of notebook paper, along with a
short message:

> *this is Josh I'm alive and I am at century correctional institu-*
> *tion I need you to set up an account with global tele link and*
> *put money on it so I can call you please. I love you.*

I waited for an opportunity when he was alone, and I went over to
his bunk. As I approached, he closed his book and kept a finger in it

so that it didn't fully close, as if he was marking his place. I assumed he was also hiding his phone because we were not friends or close, so how would I even know that he had a phone?

"Sorry to bother you," I said. "I have a problem, and I'm hoping you can help me. I haven't spoken to my family in eighteen months. I spent thirteen months in solitary confinement and then got bounced from the jail to a federal prison for a month. Then I got bounced from the reception center to the work camp, and now I'm here. I just want to let my dad know that I'm alive, let him know where I am but I can't call him because he doesn't know that he needs to put money on the phone to enable me to call him. I'm looking to shoot a text message to him and my mom and maybe get on the phone for thirty seconds or so to tell him to put money on the phone."

Sin was blank faced. "Why are you coming to me for help? What do you think I can do to help you?"

"Look, man," I replied. "I'm not stupid, and while I might be new to prison, I pay attention to what goes on around me. I see the revolving door that you have. I know that you have a phone. I get it. It's your hustle. So tell me how much I have to pay to get on the phone."

"I like you," Sin responded. "Normally, I charge five dollars per text message and twenty dollars per minute to use the phone, ten dollars to look up something simple on the internet, and twenty dollars to look up another inmate. You seem like a good dude, and you already developed a reputation for paying your debts, so I'll send a text message for you and let you get on the phone, and then you pay me after."

"Thank you," I replied as I handed him the little slip of paper with some writing on it. "Here's my mom's number and my dad's number and a message. When can I make the call?"

"When everyone goes to lunch, stay in the dorm," Sin said. "You can call then. It'll be quiet, with only one officer in the bubble."

I thanked him and walked back to my bunk.

"Chow time!" The guard shouted it twice over the loudspeaker. Most of the inmates in the dorm were already piled up at the vestibule waiting to go. With a loud click, the doors buzzed open, and like a herd of stampeding buffalo, the inmates rushed to the chow hall. About fifteen inmates remained in the dorms. Once the last straggler had left and the door slammed shut, I got up and went over to Sin's bunk. I sat on the floor next to his bunk in the same fashion that I'd seen all of the other customers do. He looked around, then handed me a phone. It was an old Nextel flip phone with real buttons, no touch screen. In 2014, who the hell even sold a phone like that?

"Thirty seconds. Make it quick," Sin said.

I called my father. The phone rang once, twice, three times. What if he didn't answer? Shit! I hadn't even thought of that. What could I do if my dad wouldn't answer because he didn't recognize the number?

"Hello?" I heard his voice answer.

"Dad, it's me, Josh." My voice broke, and I started to cry even though I was doing everything in my power to prevent it. But that voice, my father's voice, it was like a punch to the stomach, a reminder of how far away from anyone who cared about me I really was. Eighteen months—I might have forgotten the sound of my father's voice, but more than that, I had forgotten the feeling of love. A tidal wave of hopelessness and agony washed over me.

"Where are you?" he was saying. It shocked me out of the moment.

"Dad, it's so good to hear your voice." My voice cracked, and I hiccupped as I choked back more tears. "I'm in the panhandle, Century Correctional Institution. Dad, I don't have much time because I'm not supposed to be on a cell phone. I need you to set up a phone account and put money on it so that I can call you. I really need to talk to you."

I only half noticed that a black guy who was part of the group that always sat in the corner smoking and doing drugs had given me a dirty look and then gone to the guard's bubble and started talking through the flap. I didn't think anything of it, because many of the black inmates made a habit of talking to the officers, especially trying to flirt with female officers. All of a sudden three officers burst into the dorm and came running straight for Sin and me. I froze like a deer in the headlights. Phone in my hand, dDad still on the line.

"Fuck! Dad, I gotta go."

The guard, an older black sergeant, said, "Give me the phone, son. I got to take you to confinement."

Being the dumbass that I am, I handed the phone to the officer. I should have chucked it across the floor under the bunks, kicked it like a hockey puck, anything. They would still have confiscated the phone, but nobody would've been *caught* with it. But because I wasn't slick, the thought hadn't even crossed my mind.

"Turn around and cuff up," the sergeant said.

"Sarge," Sin said, "that is *my* phone. Not his."

"Then you're both going in. Him for being caught red-handed using it and you for possession of contraband. The disciplinary hearing can sort everything out."

I thought Sin was being selfless and altruistic, and I thanked him for it.

"Hey, man," I said, "I appreciate you trying to look out."

Sin just shook his head and remained silent as we were cuffed and escorted to confinement.

We arrived in administrative segregation, the part of confinement where you sit until they convict and sentence you. Sin and I were separated, and they took him through a vestibule and out of sight. Shortly after, two officers came to escort me through the same door toward the confinement cells. I heard them talking about having no choice but to put us in the same cell because they had no room.

Too many people had been caught with cell phones, fifteen already this week. They escorted me down a long hallway, grayish-blue floors and walls, prison cell after prison cell on my right, two bunks and a stainless steel toilet, and steel bars, each identical but for the different inmates in each. The smell was horrible. There was no air-conditioning, no heat, and poor ventilation. Late summer, early autumn, the heat was intense. There were sections of the walls that were actually bubbling.

I know this sounds crazy, but they paint the floors and walls with a latex-based paint, and the heat and humidity were so intense that the walls actually sweat. The latex paint prevents moisture from evaporating, so instead, the paint would bubble out until it got about the size of a beach ball, and then it would burst, dumping a couple of gallons of moisture on the floor. In confinement, the inmates only got showers twice a week if the officers were doing their jobs, less if the officers wanted to fuck with you. Add to the heat and poor ventilation, the smell of men who only get an opportunity to bathe once a week—it was sickening.

As we arrived at our destination, I found Sin already in the cell with his hands still cuffed behind his back. The officer opened the cell and pushed me inside.

"Turn around and come to the bean flap so I can uncuff you," the officer said.

After removing both of our handcuffs, the officer walked away. As soon as we heard the sound of the door shut behind the officer at the end of the hall, Sin punched me in the face.

"What the fuck, man!" I said, holding my jaw.

"We have to fight," Sin said. "That phone cost me over $1,000, and somebody has to pay for it. You're going to get your family to put $1,000 on my canteen account to cover my loss. And we're going to fight three times a day, every day until they do, or until you check in and are taken off of the compound."

"How am I supposed to communicate this to my family?" I asked. "I'm in confinement with you. There is no phone here and no way for me to get a hold of them. Also, there's no way in hell that five-dollar flip phone from the 1980s cost $1,000!"

"That's not my problem," Sin said. "I am the shot caller for all of Folk Nation on this compound. There are certain rules and expectations that I have to follow, and you have to pay for that phone. That phone was not just my phone. That phone belongs to Folk Nation. You don't just owe me—you owe every member of Folk on this whole compound. When you get out of confinement, you're going to fight every one of them until you've paid for it. You will pay for it in blood until you pay for it in cash."

"What was I supposed to do?" I asked, both exasperated and alarmed.

"Anything other than willingly give the phone to the police," Sin replied. "Throw it, fling it across the floor, shove it up your ass, and take off running, *anything!*"

"I am sorry," I said. "I didn't know. I will make it up to you, but I really do not want to fight you or anyone else."

"You don't have a choice," Sin stated matter-of-factly. "Neither of us do."

Sin threw another punch at me, and we started fighting. His heart didn't seem to be in it, and mine certainly wasn't. We hit each other in the body and face a few times, but there was nothing impressive or spectacular about our it. I hit him in the stomach with an uppercut and knocked the wind out of him, so he held up his hand to stop the fight. I stopped and stepped back. He sat on the toilet, and I sat on the bottom bunk.

As we were huffing and puffing, catching our breath, Sin said to me, "You've got heart. That's for sure. Where did you learn how to fight like that? I have never seen anyone fight the way you do, and I did Muay Thai for a few years."

"I was in the Marine Corps," I replied. "We fight. It's what we do."

"Nah," Sin said. "I fought other Marines, and they don't fight the way you do. That was something else."

I held my hands palms up. "We good now?" I asked.

"For now. We will fight again after dinner," Sin responded. "What kind of music do you like?"

The idea of making small talk between brawls just didn't make sense. This was a whole different world, a whole different culture, with a language all its own, and I was feeling like everybody I'd encountered was either absolutely crazy, completely ignorant, or off-the-charts stupid.

"Rock," I said. "Blues, jazz. Anything other than rap or country music."

"Cool," Sin says. "Pick a song."

"Why?" I reply.

"Because I cannot stand the ignorant monkeys beating on the walls and the bunks all day and all night, thinking that they're rap stars," Sin said. "I've been in prison for a long time, and this isn't my first rodeo in confinement. If I have to listen to them beating on bunks and walls with that garbage, then they have to listen to me sing. Pick a song, and we'll start singing."

"How about 'Under The Bridge,' Red Hot Chili Peppers."

"Oooh, good one," Sin replied. Then he started belting it out.

His voice was *amazing*—like *American Idol*-finalist-level good. Could this day get any weirder?

Well, it was about to.

I joined in singing with him

"Shut the fuck up with that bullshit!" someone shouted from a few cells away. "No one wants to hear that white cracker bullshit!"

Sin and I smiled at each other, and we sang louder as we got up and walked to the bars, making sure that our voices carried through the entire cellblock.

"Shut the fuck up, cracka!" the same inmate shouted again. "If you don't knock that shit off, I am going to fuck you up!"

"Bitch," Sin says loudly, "what are you going to do? You are in confinement just like us. Sit your ass down and enjoy the music."

"Sin, is that you?" another voice shouted from further down the hall.

"Yeah," Sin shouted back. "Black Boy, is that you?"

"What up, my nigga!" Black Boy shouted back. "What are you in for?"

"Cell phone," Sin replied.

"Awww, shit," Black Boy shouted. "Again? This is the third time this year for you."

"Wasn't my fault this time," Sin said. "One of the Bloods snitched because new guy came to me instead of them, and he fights really good, so they snitched instead of jumping him. What you in for?"

"Punk checked in on me," Black Boy shouted. "Said he was afraid I was gonna rape him. Dumb bitch."

"My nigga," Sin says, "You need to leave them punks alone. There are enough punks who you can pay for sex and avoid all the drama. Stop chasing every young white boy on the compound."

"You right, you right." Black Boy chuckled. "Keep singing. Sounds really good, and it's better than listening to that bug rap about raping white women and killing police. Same shit over and over, same garbage-ass beat too."

"A'ight," Sin said. "Good music coming right up!"

For the next two weeks, Sin and I fought after breakfast, after lunch, and after dinner. When we weren't fighting, we were singing rock songs from the '90s and early 2000s. We sang "The Anthem" by

Good Charlotte, and we sang "Through Glass" by Stone Sour, "Basketcase" by Green Day and "45" by Shinedown. Some of the songs I didn't know the words for, but Sin knew the words to *every* song, and he was happy to sing anything I requested. The more we sang, the less real our fights became, turning more and more playful.

One morning, Sin turned to me as we were eating breakfast and said, "I don't wanna fight you anymore, Josh. But everybody else needs to believe we *are* fighting. They can't see us, but they can hear us. So let's make it *sound* real. You got me?"

We sat on my bunk side by side and proceeded to beat on our chests with our hands, sometimes with closed fists, sometimes open hand. We worked hard to make very realistic fight sounds, and the occasional grunt, gasp, or cry of pain thrown in for good effect always sold it.

"Aw shit, there goes Josh and Sin, fighting again," someone a few cells down said.

"Sounds like a good one today."

"Sounds like Sin is winning this one! Get him, Sin!"

This worked great for a few days, but then we went to DR court. Even in prison, they make a mockery of the justice system, as any infraction has to result in a conviction before punishment can be doled out. It's a kangaroo court. You spend a few weeks being abused in confinement, then go to Disciplinary Referral Court where they "sentence" you to more time in confinement or some kind of punitive forced labor, such as mowing grass with old mechanical push mowers known as "flintstones." We were both sentenced to sixty days disciplinary confinement for possession of the cell phone.

When we got back to the cell, Sin told me that when we got back out onto the compound in two months, I was still going to owe him the money for the phone, and I'd surely get jumped by all of the other gang members in Folk Nation until I had paid it. He couldn't stop it because it was part of the code they had to abide.

The worst part was that he told me it was almost guaranteed that someone was going to stab me.

"Josh, you need to get off this compound," Sin said. "It is the *only* way you will survive."

"How does that work?" I asked. "How to I make that happen? I can't just tell them I don't want to be here anymore."

"Here's what you do," Sin said. "You need to check in on me. Tell them you fear for your life. It might not work, but if it does, it's the fastest way. They will keep me in confinement under investigation for a while, though."

"There has to be a better way," I said. "There has to be a way that doesn't involve me hurting you or getting it on record that I'm scared."

"You could always go psych," Sin said. "Tell them you're depressed or suicidal, ask for medication. This isn't a psych camp, so they'll have to transfer you somewhere where they can give you medication. It's a rough trip, and those camps are crazy."

I thought it over long and hard.

"That's what I'll do."

The next time an officer came for count, I ask him for a request form to speak to the psych doctor. After he brought the form, I filled it out talking about wanting to get on medication for anxiety and depression and turned it in. The next day, someone from medical came and spoke with me, trying to talk me out of asking for psych meds and making sure I understood the consequences of moving forward with this, include being transferred to a facility specifically designed for crazy inmates. I was terrified because he made it sound really intimidating, but I pushed forward. I knew I had no choice. The medic told me that I would still have to serve my sixty days in confinement, but that I would be transferred to a psych camp within three days.

On the afternoon of my last day at Century as we were finishing lunch, Sin started choking. He was grabbing his throat and started turning purple. At first, I thought he was faking because he had a sick sense of humor, but when he fell to the ground, I realized something serious was happening. I pulled him up and got behind him. Making my right hand into a fist, I wrapped my arms around him and put my fist just below his sternum. I grabbed my fist with my other hand and started performing the Heimlich. It took a few tries, but suddenly, a dark brown chunk of what was an imitation-meat patty flew out of his mouth as he gasped for air.

"You just saved my life," Sin said, gasping. "You could have let me die and…you'd have been…free of your debt to me. Why did you save me?"

"You were choking," I replied. "It was the right thing to do."

"You saved my life," Sin said, "You saved my life for no reason. You have saved the life of a member of Folk Nation. You do not want to be in a gang, but you're better than that. You are now Friend Of Folk. You are now 606."

"What does that mean?" I ask. "606?"

"F is the sixth letter of the alphabet." Sin says. "606 is the highest honor that an outsider can have with us. It means that we will have your back if you need us—all the benefits of being a member, none of the obligation. We owe you a life debt."

Sin walked to the bars of the cell and shouted for the entire wing to hear, "Josh is now 606. As a Friend of Folk, we have his back. Fuck with Josh, you fuck with Folk Nation." Then he turned to me and said, "Good luck with the rest of your bid, man. Stay away from phones, gambling, gays, and guards, and you'll be all right."

ACI- SEAGULLS AND SUGAR DADDIES

After my debacle with Sin, I was transferred to the worst psych camp in the state—Apalachee Correctional Institution. Now I'd get to see whether Ben was telling me the truth about the seagulls.

As we drove onto the ACI compound, I noticed that the surrounding areas look like farmland and airplane runways. That didn't make any sense. Everywhere you looked, you saw old Quonset huts and airplane hangars and structures that look more like World War II military housing than prison facilities. Turns out the place had been a World War II airbase, which was cool, but we went through the same intake process that we did at every other facility here: stripped naked, bent over at the waist, cheeks spread, squat and cough, lift your dick, lift your balls, go to laundry and get issued sheets and blankets, then head to your dorm.

Still, the unusual layout, the hills and valleys surrounding these strange multistory buildings with an unusual amount of windows and entrances was hypnotizing. So many windows boarded up with plywood—the place looked like it had been condemned, and maybe it should have been. Later, I learned the place *had* been condemned—because of mold, asbestos, and other structural safety issues, and, hilariously, for a time it was even listed on the Department of Corrections website as *no longer in use.*

No longer in use? There were over twelve hundred of us inmates on the property!

Everything about ACI was different—confusing or questionable. My dorm was over 150 feet long, fifty feet wide, with bathrooms and showers at the far end in direct line of sight from every bunk in the dorm. Absolutely zero privacy. There were no bunk beds. Every bed was a single, with eight rows of beds, twenty beds deep, head to foot with a center aisle running from the guard station to the showers. Whereas all the other compounds generally have sixty to eighty inmates, this dorm had approximately 150. The boarded-up windows meant it would be brutally hot in the summer as there were no state-run prisons in Florida that had air-conditioning. Slow-moving fans were all you got in the way of circulation and ventilation. And unlike the other compounds, this dorm had ceilings so high it felt like a warehouse. The fans were so high up there that they were useless, and only half were working anyway. Plus, the bathrooms had no partitions of any kind between any of the toilets or urinals, not even the half walls between each toilet that I enjoyed elsewhere.

But the surroundings weren't the only thing that were different.

At the foot of my bunk, an inmate talked to himself, pacing back and forth with a colostomy bag creeping out of his uniform.

And on the other side of my bunk sat a short, fat, white kid who looked like Bobby from *King of the Hill.*

"Hey, buddy, what's his deal," I said. "Is he OK?"

"Don't pay him any attention," he replied. "He's harmless. Going home in six months. He wears the colostomy bag because someone stabbed him. All that pacing pisses people off."

Just then, the strangest creature I ever saw walked into the dorm, with a face like the Green Goblin, massive double-D breasts, a narrow waist, and hips and buttocks like two oversize beach balls–in uniform pants two sizes too small, and a uniform shirt three sizes too small. Four black Muslims in Kufi skullcaps, carrying copies of the Quran, circled the creature, fawning over it like puppy dogs.

Later, I learned that the Muslim Brotherhood was flagged as a criminal organization, a gang, and a hate group—just like the Aryan Brotherhood, Folk Nation, Bloods, Crips, and Latin Kings.

I turned to Bobby. "Yo, what the fuck is that thing? I didn't think women were allowed in a men's prison?"

"That," Bobby said, "is no woman. That is a man with a nine-inch cock. He was the one all over the news pretending to be a doctor while actually practicing medicine without a license. He was doing face, breast, and butt injections using rubber cement down in Miami. Somebody died as a result. It was all over the news for months. Didn't you hear about it?"

"Yeah," I said, "I vaguely recall that."

"Although it has tits like a woman," Bobby says, "that thing is not a woman. And although everyone calls it 'Auntie,' it is no one's aunt. Pay attention. There is a one-hour window everyday where these punks have exclusive use of the showers, and that…thing showers with them. Do not get in the shower during that time."

"Thanks for the heads-up."

Walking to the chow hall the next day, I saw the biggest seagulls of my life. They were the size of Labrador retrievers, and they were relentless, absolutely fearless in their pursuit of inmates who had food. These gulls had an uncanny ability to know exactly which inmate was trying to leave the chow hall with food, including those who were leaving while they were still chewing.

So it was true! Ben was not making this up!

Well, other inmates had said that today was biscuits-and-gravy day, so I was about to find out if Ben was making that up too.

I waited in the chow line, trying to discreetly check out the trays of other inmates. You couldn't look directly at them or their food because "eyeballing" was grounds for a fight. To this day, I do not fully understand why, but I guess it has something to do with dominance, submission, and the predator/prey mindset. In fast glances, I managed to get a good look at a couple of trays, and—yes!—the biscuits were *humungous*, bigger than tennis balls. Not quite as big as a softball, but close. And the trays were loaded with gravy! This was a feast!

Well, not really. Prison food would always still be prison food, neither satisfying nor nutritious, all starch and carbs without any protein or nutrients, and absolutely disgusting by even so-called Third World standards. But wow! At least I would be full for a while—maybe for the first time in a year and a half.

By the way, according to the Florida Department of Corrections website regarding inmate meals, "The menu, including portion sizes, is specifically designed to meet the caloric requirements for moderately active adults and is reviewed and approved by a registered dietitian. The menu currently provides an average of 2,762 calories per day."

This is a boldfaced lie, almost comical. Any person who has been incarcerated in Florida at any point since the year 2000 can assure you that the calories per day average less than fifteen hundred. Many of us managed to get our hands on dietary books from the American Heart Association and the American Diabetes Association that break down the caloric content of nearly all foods available for consumption. For those inmates who eat Kosher, the foods actually have the calorie and nutrition facts on the packaging, totaling less than twelve hundred per day, unless you include the Kool-Aid packets, seven hundred empty, nutritionless calories nobody needs.

Being completely sedentary, reading and sleeping all day, eating everything on your tray, you still lose weight and are hungry all the time. Reconstituted dehydrated potatoes, a textured vegetable-protein patty, boiled cabbage, and three Jell-o cubes was the normal meal served. There were some variations, of course. For instance, sometimes instead of the reconstituted potatoes, they would substitute bleached pasta or bleached rice. During the summer, we might get boiled squash instead of boiled cabbage. I had a chance to work in the kitchens at Century, and I can tell you that I will never again eat squash that I have not prepared for myself. Why, you may ask? Because I watched grown men cut one end off of the squash and then have sex with it. And every one of those squash and zucchini that had been raped and impregnated by inmates were then cut and served to the general inmate population.

But I digress.

The important thing is Ben was right!

They fed you here; your tray got filled. Nothing healthy, nothing nutritious, but it was food.

On my first full day, I had to go to Classification to receive my job assignment. I still don't know how job assignments were determined, but I was thrilled when they put me in the carpentry trade school on the compound. This would give me the opportunity to learn something while also keeping my mind busy—anything so I wouldn't dwell on how horrible my life had become and how hopeless my future looked.

I got back to the dorm, excited to tell Bobby. Goofy as he was, Bobby was relatively intelligent not medicated, and really the only person that I had to talk to at that point. I had only just arrived, after all.

When I got back to my bunk, I noticed that my little spastic neighbor was in rare form. He was pacing back and forth in a frenzy, intense and determined. He was also muttering to himself frantically, almost arguing with himself. The colostomy back was swinging wildly as he paced: *Step, step, pivot. Step, step, pivot.*

Bobby, on the other hand, was nowhere to be seen.

Maybe he was on the yard or in the canteen line. All of a sudden Spaz grabbed a walking cane from the old man a few bunks away and marched determinedly across the dorm to a stocky Latin guy built like a brick house. It was like schizophrenic David going up against Goliath. The Latin man was sitting on his bunk reading the Bible, as Spaz-man marched up and swung the cane down like a sledgehammer right onto his head.

Oh no! He did not just do that!

You'd think I'd have been horrified, but the truth was, I was ready for a good show—bring me the popcorn.

Strange, too, to reflect now that I was already so inoculated against hardcore violence after only eighteen months incarcerated, but that's how it was.

Goliath jumped up, three times as wide and at least a foot taller than Spaz. As Spaz reared back to swing the cane again, Goliath grabbed it, yanked it right out of Spaz's hands, and used it to hit Spaz in the head. He hit Spaz so hard that the cane broke in half, and Spaz collapsed to the ground.

The show was over fast, and all us onlookers couldn't help being a little disappointed, but then—

Goliath took the broken cane and stabbed it down into the Spaz's chest like he was staking a vampire. My God, I could hear the suction sound as he pulled the broken cane out, watched Spaz's body arch up and then plop back down on the ground as the cane-stake pulled free. Someone should have done something. Not me, though, I had just gotten there, and I didn't know the backstories—no way was I jumping into the fray.

Again and again, Goliath drove the cane into Spaz's chest. Again and again, I heard the suction sounds as his body arched then plopped onto the ground. When the piece of cane was too bloody for Goliath to hold, he dropped it and grabbed the other piece.

Goliath drove the cane fragment down into his *eye*!

That's when I knew I was witnessing a murder, sheer brutality, Mortal Kombat–level gore.

One, two, three times into the eye. One, two, three times into the throat. Suddenly, the cane fragment broke. Goliath stood up, grabbed Spaz by the ankle, and dragged him across the dorm to the shower. Once in the shower, Goliath started punching Spaz. I don't know how many times he punched him, as there was a half wall blocking my view, but I could hear it—*thwack thwack, thwack, thwack*!

When would this end? Where were the guards? Why was no one helping? Why was *I* not helping? I was tired of trouble, tired of fighting, but someone should have been helping!

Why were there no guards?

Goliath turned on the shower, walked back to his bunk, got soap, towel, and clean uniforms. I watched as he walked back to the shower, took a full shower, and was dressed and dried on his bunk reading the Bible—yeah, his *Bible*—before any guards came on the scene. They wheeled Spaz out on a gurney, and a helicopter arrived not long after to take him to the nearest civilian hospital. I have no idea if he made it, but I cannot imagine he survived. Poor kid, less than six months to freedom. The guards handcuffed Goliath, who complied without fuss. They took him out of the dorm, and I never saw him again.

Bobby got back to the dorm not long after. I told him about it, and he was nonplussed, completely unfazed. I guessed that I had to adopt that mentality too in order to survive, but if I was being honest, I didn't think I could ever unsee what I saw, and I never wanted to see anything like it again, not ever.

The next day, I started the carpentry program. The teacher was Mr. Chamberlain. To get to the class, I walked past trees, something that just didn't exist on regular prison compounds. They didn't exist here either, but the carpentry program was down a hill, separated by multiple gates, fences, and a metal detector.

When I walked into the shop, I was blown away. This was not prison. This was the real thing—table saws, band saws, grinders, belt sanders, routers, drill press, chisels, wooden sticks and boards, dowel rods, paint, paint thinner, and more. Plus, there were no guards, not a single one on this side of the fence. Apparently, they allowed a bunch of dangerous criminals to operate power tools and saws unsupervised. I mean, we were not totally unsupervised. The teacher was here, but still, he was just a civilian with a walkie-talkie, not an officer.

I was so excited to be doing normal things in a normal setting like a normal human. Yeah, I had to go back to prison at the end of every day, but for six hours a day, I did not *feel* like I was in prison.

I started to become more hopeful, and some of the darkness receded. This made the time go by faster and distracted me enough to forget that I was in prison for just a few hours per day. That is, until the weekend arrived. On the weekend, there was no carpentry, no activity. There was nothing but a dorm full of mentally ill criminals and a ton of homosexuals having sex with each other. I'm not homophobic. I have gay friends, and I'm happy for them when they get married or have positive relationships. However, I did not want to walk into the bathroom at 2:00 a.m. to urinate and stumble over two men having anal sex over a toilet, creating a sickening stench you can never forget it once you have smelled it.

Needless to say, I did walk into the bathroom at 2:00 a.m. to urinate on this particular Saturday night, and there was a bedsheet tied to a broom and to a plastic spoon shoved into a crack in the wall, so that the person on the back toilet could have privacy to shit or masturbate. In either case, I paid it no attention and used the urinal. Suddenly. the smell hit me in the face like a punch from Mike Tyson. and I gagged.

The sound of my gagging startled the men who were on the toilet behind the sheet. In that moment, one of the men, a young, scrawny boy eighteen years old with glasses and a vulture-like neck, a guy everyone called Chicken Little, knocked the broom over. As the broom fell and the sheet collapsed, it revealed an overweight black man with a congenital birth defect that affected one arm. Everyone called him Chicken Wing. His pants were around his ankles, and he had an erection that rivaled the Empire State Building. He was stand-ing facing the toilet as if he were pissing in it, and Chicken Little was bent over at the waist with one hand on the wall and one hand on the seat of the toilet. Chicken Little had his pants around his ankles, and there was blood and feces on his ass and the back of his legs. He was silently crying, but that was not stopping Chicken Wing from thrusting his hips forward and back like a jackhammer. This shocked me from half asleep to fully awake, and I recognized clearly that this man in his forties was raping this eighteen-year-old boy with what amounted to a full-size Maglite flashlight.

As the boy shook his head silently, Chicken Wing whispered to me through clenched teeth, "If you say a word, I'll fuck you too."

I decided not to get involved. Whatever they had going on was their business, and anyway, the kid shook his head no, like he didn't want help. I had already been informed that Chicken Wing had HIV, and fighting him was not a risk worth taking. I was not about to pick up HIV in prison because I chose to get involved in what could have been an intimate moment between lovers, just because it *looked* like rape to me.

Back to beddy-bye for me.

Still, guilt kept me awake the rest of the night, and as soon as I got my breakfast tray, I handed it to a random person and walked out of the chow hall. I couldn't eat. I wanted to talk to the boy and make sure he was OK, wanted to report the rape, wanted to make sure it *was* in fact rape, and not rough sex between pals.

When the dorm was released for rec, I saw an opportunity to approach Chicken Little discreetly. I looked for him on the rec yard, saw him walking gingerly, and when he got to a relatively isolated area, I followed.

"Hey," I said, "are you OK?"

His eyes went wide for a second, then I saw shame flash across his face briefly. "Yes. I'm *fine*. A little uncomfortable is all."

"You need to report it? Rape is not OK, and it is not your fault."

"Rape?" Chicken Little said, almost laughing. "That wasn't rape. Chicken Wing is my war daddy."

"Your...*war daddy*?"

"Yeah. Like a sugar daddy. Except instead of paying me for sex, I pay him for protection."

"Excuse me," I replied, "you pay him for protection against getting raped, by letting him rape you? I don't understand."

"I don't have any money to pay him," Chicken Little says. "So I give him my ass and my mouth as payment in exchange for protection. Better that it's one person of my choosing than a variety of people against my will when I'm not ready."

"That's not OK," I said. "Fifty rapists or one rapist, it's not acceptable. You don't need to pay for protection. Just stand up for yourself. Fight. Stab someone if needed. It doesn't even matter if you win or lose, just that you're willing to stand up for yourself. Getting beat up is not nearly as bad as getting raped. Plus, he has HIV."

But Chicken Little was scowling. "Just mind your own business!"

As he limped away, I realized that I was glad I had not interfered—the guilt that had been weighing me down all night was gone in a flash.

A few months after my arrival, the weather got really cold. The panhandle on the border of Georgia and Alabama was much colder than South Florida. A few days were below twenty degrees, and at least one day was below fifteen. Ice covered the grass, not just a little frost but hard, crusty ice. There was ice on the sidewalk, and some inmates slipped and fell, so the officers blocked it off and forced us to walk on the grass (which was absolutely prohibited at all other times). We were not allowed to have any kind of beanie or skull cap, no gloves or scarves. The same uniform that we wore the rest of the year was the uniform we had to wear through the winter. Prison uniforms are almost identical to hospital scrubs, only with a rougher, more abrasive material, and not really any warmer. The so-called jackets we were issued had no linings, no insulation, and were made of the same scrub material. It was like putting a second shirt on, which only helped to break some of the wind chill but did nothing to keep you warm.

This was ironic, since the cellblocks were sweltering in summer, unbearable at 120 degrees and up, even when it was only ninety-eight to a hundred degrees outside. The heat was suffocating for weeks at a time, and the officers would do everything in their power to ensure that we spent as much time inside as possible. They had a million excuses as to why we couldn't go to the rec yard, to the canteen, to the library or the chapel. Count times sometimes exceeded two hours, and we stood there, wearing multiple layers, silent. During the winter, when it was warm in the dorms and below freezing outside, they made us go out to rec every day, the count times generally lasted less than twenty minutes, and they kicked us out of the dorms every chance they got. They didn't want us gravitating to any other warmer location, so chapel services and library were often cancelled for a myriad of preposterous reasons—anything to make sure we stood in line in wide-open, windy, freezing weather. If we put our hands in our pants to warm them up, they'd throw us in confinement for "gunning," i.e., masturbating in public.

The absurdity was creeping up on me, slowly but surely. I had never given it much thought before, but big questions were arising. Wasn't prison supposed to be a place where criminals were reformed? Where people who had taken a wrong path were taught a better way to act and treat people? Wasn't the idea to help us change and then release us into society to be law-abiding citizens?

If that was the idea, something was very wrong. The primary purpose of prison was to box criminals up, kind of like a human warehouse, a barracks to keep them away from society. The only problem was, this meant that, once the prisoner had been boxed up for a period of time, you had to release him out into the world, angrier, more violent, more skilled at burglary, more able to pull off sleight of hand, more of a crooked con than ever before.

Florida Statute 20.315 regarding the organizational structure and mission of the Department of Corrections states that the goals of the department shall be

> *(a). To protect society by providing incarceration that will support the intentions of established criminal law;*

> *(b). To ensure that inmates work while they are incarcerated and that the department makes every effort to collect restitution and other monetary assessments from the inmates while they are incarcerated or under supervision.*

And yet we did not get paid for working in prison. Florida eliminated that little part before I was even born. Instead, if we *didn't* work, our sentence got extended. We were awarded two days per month gain time. This was supposedly time off of our sentence for good behavior, totaling twenty-four days a year but which may not reduce our time served below 80 percent of the original sentence. The day-to-day rules, if you can call them that, were entirely arbitrary and 100 percent at the whim of the officers. Female officers could extend your sentence if they thought you were flirting with them, if you smiled at them, or if you didn't flirt with them or didn't smile at them. It was like a game of Russian roulette designed by Kafka.

One thing I learned: The power to dominate others comes with a great risk. When you have eighty-plus mentally unstable men in one room, most with decades of time ahead of them and nothing to lose, and it's below freezing outside, an officer can only push his or her power so far. And if *they* cross the line?

You got a riot.

It happened just after Thanksgiving, just after dinner chow ended.

"Hey," someone shouted, "they *bucking* next door! They bucking!"

As I glanced up from the book I was reading, I saw what looked like a massive barroom brawl taking place in the dorm across the courtyard. Trash cans were being thrown, beds were being flipped, paper flying, inmates jumping, running around.

It was terrible, and it was beautiful.

The loudspeaker blasted: "On your bunks! On your bunks! Everyone on your bunks now!" Most everyone complied, but everyone was paying attention to what was going on in the other dorm. How could they not? It was like watching pay-per-view, but for free and in real life. Someone went flying past a window, then another someone, then another. This continued for a few minutes, until a group of guards walked up. *Walking*? Yes, casually. They didn't even care that a riot was going on. Two of them had riot shields, two had shotguns, and two had assault rifles. Don't ask me why. A bunch of innocent men were going to be murdered tonight, and the Department of Corrections was going to cover it up. If it was bad enough to bring in guns, they should have called in the National Guard. The guards just stood there outside the dorm, though. Why didn't they enter? What were they waiting for? More inmates to murder each other like Goliath and Spaz? Truth be told, I was surprised to find myself still shocked—you'd think I'd have learned by now just how corrupt most of these guards were—beyond any inmates, any criminals. Coming face to face with prison guards, I honestly felt that I had experienced what few can say they have faced: *true evil*, the power to abuse with impunity.

Funnily enough, there's a quote I don't know the source of. Some say Churchill said it. Some say Ben Franklin. Actually, it doesn't matter who said it, because it remains the truest line I have ever heard: "Anyone wishing to witness true corruption must merely sit in the nearest prison parking lot at shift change."

After about thirty minutes, the guards finally entered the dorm. A few moments later, two of the guards exited with a third guard between them as if he was injured and they were helping him walk, but I could see that his feet were dragging on the ground. He was completely unconscious. Still, somehow, the guards managed to quell the riot, and throughout the rest of the evening and into the night, they were taking inmates out of the dorm in handcuffs. The day after next, nearly fifty new inmates were brought into that dorm, meaning they shipped all the rioters to other compounds like cattle.

* * *

All this time, I loved working in the woodshop, loved the feeling of sawdust on my hands, the smell of cedar. I discovered that I had a natural talent for carpentry, especially on the scroll saw. I was surprised to learn that I had the patience and the steady hands necessary to create detailed works—at first, they were simple shapes like circles and stars, but in no time, I was pulling off three-dimensional shadow box cutouts of tigers prowling through the jungle and wooden toys for children. I was not as good at finish work—I got heavy-handed with the polyurethane varnish, but it was joyous to make something.

And it took me back, back to '97, Cape Cod, visiting Papa and Grammy, my mom's folks. They were hard people. My grandmother could talk more than anyone I had ever met in my life—in fact, she was only person I've ever met who could fall asleep in the middle of a sentence, wake up forty-five minutes later and continue right where she left off. Papa was a strong man, tall and stoic, my favorite person in the world, and though I was always intimidated by him, I really loved our time together. He served in the Army Air Corps during World War II, back before the Air Force was formed. I didn't know it at the time, but he sold plumbing parts for a living, and he was a phenomenal craftsman and artist. Their entire house on the Cape was filled with high-quality handmade furniture, his beautiful paintings framed all over the walls, and finely crafted cutouts—a chunk of Noah's Ark with all of the animals on each level of the boat. Outside was beautiful too—handcrafted birdhouses of many different styles peppered the garden.

Papa's workshop was in the basement. Even at six or seven, he'd let me in there to try things, and he was incredibly gentle and patient with me, as we used scroll saws and table saws to build my first birdhouse. It was so simple, but to me, it was the most beautiful ever, and Papa was so proud of me, so full of praise. He was especially proud that I had an idea that we should put a trap door on the bottom of the birdhouse so that we could open it and empty out the old nests and debris and let new families move in year after year.

How had I come from there to here?

I'd stopped looking at my calendar and counting days, stopped counting the weeks and months. In the back of my head, I knew that I had about four years remaining on my sentence, but as soon as I found something to occupy my time, I no longer felt the need to monitor. In fact, *not* counting the days actually made them go by faster. Days turned into weeks and months while you weren't looking.

It's funny. I valued my time in the carpentry shop so much that anytime I saw another inmate doing something that could jeopardize the program, I got aggressive with them. The policy was such that if one person smuggled something from the carpentry shop onto the main compound, if one person got caught making a weapon or doing something stupid or dangerous, then all twelve of us were going to go to confinement and get banned from participation in any vocational programs. No way was I going to let that happen.

One morning, I saw one of the inmates rapping, using a table saw as a drum kit. I knew that the particular table saw had a faulty on/off switch and, if jarred too hard, could turn on without warning.

"Hey, yo!" I said. "Save that ignorant ghetto shit for the dorm. You can get us all locked up doing that shit down here. If that saw turns on and somebody gets hurt, we're all going to jail!"

"Shut the fuck up, pussy-ass cracker bitch!" the inmate said. "I do what I want, and I'll fuck up anybody who thinks they can tell me otherwise! Punk-ass white boy!"

It might be important to note that I was *constantly* slurred for being white—but if I were so insane as to call someone a punk-ass black boy or some such, I would surely be jumped and murdered *inside the hour*.

And so, instead of name-calling, I picked up two dowel rods, each approximately two feet long, roughly one inch in diameter. They felt perfectly natural in my hands, like two kali—escrima arnis sticks.

"I will give you what you're looking for, fuck nugget," I said. "If it saves everyone from getting kicked out of the carpentry program, I'm happy to take one for the team."

The other inmate ducked down behind a piece of equipment so that he was hidden from the teacher's office.

He started shouting, "I'll fuck you up, bitch, fucking pussy-ass bitch! I'm gonna break your fucking knees!"

Of course, hearing all the shouting brought the teacher out of his office, and there I was, directly in his line of sight holding two pieces of wood like weapons.

"Bork!" he said. "Outside, now!"

"But, sir—"

"I don't want to hear it. Outside, now!"

As I walked outside, the teacher pushed his panic button and then got on a walkie-talkie to some of the officers, requesting an immediate security detail to escort me to confinement.

The officers came, unceremoniously handcuffed me, and escorted me to confinement, where I sat for a few weeks before going to DR court. I was found guilty of some bizzaro made-up infraction and sentenced to two weeks on the DR squad, a fancy word for forced labor, pushing *Flintstones*-era lawnmowers. These rusty things had no motors and incredibly dull blades, nothing like the riding mowers the regular gardening crew had, but I knew that was the point: brutal physical labor as punishment. I didn't care. The bigger issue was that I'd been assigned to a different dorm, and much of my personal belongings were now missing, taken by whichever inmate packed up my stuff for the officers.

Nice.

The dorm that I was assigned to was in the opposite wing of the same building, aka the kitchen dorm. Most of the inmates here were absent for half of the day, and the rest tended to be absent the other half. The fact that it was a working dorm made it a more peaceful place because everyone had *something* to occupy their minds and their time. There was a small group of guys who played a very weird game every Saturday, all sitting around the steel table in the common area with papers and pencils and unusual dice. How they managed to get their hands on dice, I'll never know. I was curious about the game, so I walked up and watched on my first Saturday in the dorm.

"Hey," I said, "what are you playing?"

"Dungeons & Dragons," a young, slightly heavyset guy said. "Would you like to join us?" He was very well-spoken, obviously educated.

"Dungeons & Dragons?" I replied, sarcasm dripping from my voice. "That's gay."

They were totally unfazed and resumed playing their game. Their game didn't make any sense to me. I told myself I'd stick to chess, a game with clear-cut rules that I could actually win.

The following week, though, I saw the same group of guys playing Dungeons & Dragons again. This time, I noticed that the players were all young, white guys. The mentality in prison was that only child molesters played Dungeons & Dragons, and also that every white guy in prison was probably in prison for molesting little boys. This was, of course, not the case, but what was true was that the only people I had met who played Dungeons & Dragons tended to be college graduates, more highly educated people with a love for philosophy, intellectual pursuits, creativity, and so forth. Makes sense, given that the rules are expansive and technical, and that the material you must learn is vast. My understanding of the situation started to change: It wasn't that all white guys were child molesters and only child molesters played D&D. Rather, D&D was mostly played by the educated, and unfortunately, in prison, that generally excludes people of color.

Still, I had a bad attitude. Every time I'd walk past their table, I'd mutter, "Gay," or some other snide remark.

Finally, the same guy who had invited me turned in his chair. "Dude," he said, "I would *really* like it if you stopped insulting us."

"Yeah, well," I said, "I really like women. Looks like neither of us is getting what we want today."

To my surprise, he was unfazed. "OK, then," he said. "I see you playing chess, like, every day. How about a bet?"

He had me, dead to rights.

"OK," I replied. "What kind of bet did you have in mind?

"Five games. And if you win all five? You can make fun of us all you want—*and we will take it*. But if I beat you, even once, you have to play Dungeons & Dragons with us just *one time*."

I probably laughed in his face. Talk about a piece of cake. Even if I lost a game, which I wouldn't, there was no real cost except a few hours of my day. I mean, so what? I didn't exactly have visitors kicking down the gate to see me.

"You got a deal," I said. "My name is Josh, and today is the day that you are going to get your ass handed to you in the game of chess. Try not to cry, because I *will* laugh at you."

He smiled and extended a hand to shake. "Deal—but when you have to play Dungeons & Dragons with us—and you will—you are not allowed to enjoy yourself. My name is Trevor, and today is the day you lose."

He introduced himself with the same polite formality that was used in *The Princess Bride*: "Hello. My name is Inigo Montoya. You killed my father. Prepare to die"

We broke out the chessboard and started to play with his geeky crew gathered around. Setting up the pieces took longer than game one did.

"Checkmate," I said. "Four moves. You sure you want to be embarrassed four more times?"

"I cannot believe I let you beat me with 'fool's mate,'" Trevor said. "It will not happen again."

Game two, three, and four took a bit longer than the first as Trevor was actually a pretty good player. I had never seen him play, so I made the incorrect assumption that he just didn't know how.

"Not bad," I said. "But that's four and zero. You ready to cry?"

"You forget," Trevor replies, "I still have one more chance to beat you. And I am not holding back this time."

We played, and it was a good game. Trevor countered every one of my offensive moves, until he suddenly said, "Stalemate."

"Huh?" I was in shock—how could this have happened? I didn't win?

"Well," Trevor said, a little downcast, "technically, I didn't beat you, so I guess you can keep making fun of us."

"Incorrect," I responded. "The bet was that I would beat you five games in a row. Far as I am concerned, a stalemate is still a loss. While you didn't win, I did lose. I am a man of my word." I sighed. "I'll play D&D with you next Saturday."

Trevor's face visibly brightened, and he stood a little straighter.

"OK! We'll get with you over the next few days to help you get your character set up. Do you have any idea what kind of character you want to play? What race and class?"

"Um," I sheepishly replied, "I don't have any idea what the hell you're talking about."

Trevor was eager to explain this to me now. "So you have to pick a race. That is pretty self-explanatory. Elf, human, dwarf, halfling, half orc. Then you pick a class; that is what you do—wizard, sorcerer, cleric, fighter, rogue, paladin, monk, barbarian. But we already have a barbarian, sorcerer, and rogue, so you're better off picking a fighter or a monk or something similar."

"Monk?" I said. "Is that like a kung fu monk or like a religious monk?"

"Kung fu!" Trevor said with a smile.

"OK, I want to be an elf monk with two kukri swords," I said. "And I think it would be badass for it to be a female kicking ass."

As I walked away, I practically blushed. What the hell did I just get myself into? Oh man. I was turning into a nerd.

How does one survive prison as a nerd?

As it turned out, Trevor was college educated. So were the other players—Rod, Ryan, and Steven. The dungeon master (narrator, storyteller, and referee) was a college graduate and an army veteran who served in Iraq. Maybe this wasn't going to be so bad after all. I later learned that Rod was in for raping an underage girlfriend of his teen daughter, Trevor was in for possession of child porn, Ryan was in for solicitation and sexual assault of an underaged boy, and Steven, the army veteran, was in for possession of LSD. Mostly fit the prison stereotype for the gay child molester thing. Fuck.

We started in the morning before lunch and continued all the way through bedtime, around ten in the evening, and I had to admit I had a blast.

"OK, guys," I said. "Thanks for including me. Same time next week?"

"You don't have to play again," Trevor said. "You are a man of your word, a man of honor. You upheld your end of the deal."

"But I really had fun," I said. "I really want to keep playing."

"Well then," Trevor says, "welcome aboard!"

Since I'd been kicked out of the carpentry program, Classification decided that a good alternative was to put me to work in the kitchen. I was not happy. The kitchen was hard work with no reward except extra food, and I had to get up really early for the a.m. shift. I put up with it, though, because it kept me busy and the kitchen guard was pretty laid back. The civilian who ran the kitchen was not cool, though, and he never stopped hitting on me and screaming at me like I was his wife.

One morning, he started screaming at me about the way I was handling the spoon.

"You must *shake* the spoon!" he screamed. "You're giving them too much food!"

"I'm not going to shake the spoon," I said. "I'm not going to be the reason they go hungry. I have to live with them. *You don't.* You want me to work, I'm going to feed everyone. Make more food."

"I will write you up!" he shouted. "I will push the panic button and tell them you are threatening me!"

I picked up an empty steel serving pan, six inches deep and three feet long. I looked him in the eyes, then looked to the officer.

"Sarge," I said, "I have a lot of time ahead of me, and if this faggot screams at me one more time, I will break this steel pan against his head. Get this bitch right before I make you do a bunch of paperwork."

I was always respectful of the officers, even when they were dickheads. Somehow, I had managed to earn this particular officer's respect while also ensuring that he understood I was here because I had hospitalized one of his kind. It might also have been because he was one of the soldiers in the National Guard that I had been training. Who can say? He responded by grabbing the civilian by the back of the elbow and escorting him away.

"I really do not want to do paperwork today," he told the civilian, "and that inmate will hurt you. Leave him alone."

In the beginning of April 2016, my name was called for mail. This was a shocker. I didn't get any mail, no one wrote me, and no one ever responded to my letters. I walked to the officer's station to pick up the envelope, and when I looked at the return address, I realized that it was from my father.

Why was I getting a letter from him? Why now?

He had ignored me for nearly two solid years. Dark foreboding swept over me as I pull the letter out of the envelope.

Joshua,

It is with a sad heart that I must tell you Bubbe passed away....

I couldn't read the rest. My eyes filled with tears, and I collapsed to the floor, in front of everyone. I started wailing, on my knees, in the middle of the dorm. Everything else disappeared. My grief was overwhelming. I thought the pain was bad when Maddie left or when I lost Abby. That was nothing compared to this. I felt like a cannonball had exploded through my chest, leaving ragged space where my heart used to be. My *bubbe*, my grandmother. Gone. Her wisdom never again to be heard, her cooking never again to be tasted, the love, light, and warmth that always emanated from her. All at once, the world lost some color.

I felt someone put his arm under mine around my back and pick me up. I briefly registered it was Trevor. He was making me walk to my bunk, carrying me more than anything else.

I sat on my bunk and stared into space for hours, days, eternity.

The following morning, officers tried to get me to go work in the kitchen, but I was not responsive. I just sat there, crying. The officer called for backup—a few goons and a sergeant came in to force me to go to work under threat of confinement. Most of the dorm was sleeping, but this was enough of a commotion to wake a few. I barely heard what they were saying. Someone, maybe Trevor, told them there'd been a death in my family, and they left me alone, with tears streaming down my face.

After a couple days, I had recovered enough to communicate. I had generally tried to avoid the chapel because the chaplain was a homosexual whose attention really made me uncomfortable. Stranger danger, right? But in this moment, however, I went to speak to him—he granted me a short phone call to my father. And when I say short, I mean less than sixty seconds. It was just enough for me to ask my dad if she suffered and if he could please send me her obituary. Then the chaplain took the phone away and hung up on my father.

The guy didn't even extend an "I am sorry for your loss." He did, however, tell me that I had to return to work, and that he was not allowed to authorize more than forty-eight hours work exemption.

"Chaplain," I said, "I am a Jew. We sit *shiva* for seven days. It is my religious duty to spend seven days mourning the loss of my family member, and you can throw me in confinement before I minimize how important she was to me and how intense my grief is."

Suddenly, it was not an issue to write me a pass for a week of no work.

When I got back to the dorm, a large black man said something derogatory about my bubbe, about me crying like a white cracker bitch.

I was about to pick up the cane of the man who slept next to me and beat him to death with it.

Instead, I picked up my Bible and turned to Psalms, David's poems of love and loss.

DAD AND
DANGEROUS MUSIC

One morning, out of the blue, I was told to pack my stuff and get ready to transfer to the west unit. I had heard it was nicer, little to no violence, with a better rec yard, less dickish officers, and so on.

Why not?

I was excited to get away from this house of horrors.

Walking onto the new compound, my very first thought was that the west unit looked more like a college campus than a prison; all of the buildings were laid out around a quad, a large rectangular central courtyard with trees and grass in the center.

Trees that you could walk up to and touch.

I almost couldn't see the razor wire around the trunk about eight feet up.

Still, there were no boarded-up windows and very little chain link, except around the outside perimeter of the compound.

The moment I walked into my new dorm, I felt more comfortable and safer than I had in a long time. There were a group of guys in the corner near my bunk playing Dungeons & Dragons, and they had all the books you needed to pull off a full game! This was especially thrilling because those books are on the banned book list, a list drawn up by the Department of Corrections to keep inmates from learning martial arts and bomb-making. Don't ask me why a fantasy game guide was on that list. Especially when you consider that most people who play D&D are nerdy and socially awkward, hence the D&D stereotype of an obese, acne-riddled man with a lisp, living in his mother's basement.

No matter, the books were here, and the dorm was cleaner than any that I'd been in so far. Even the officer was polite and mellow. I went to my bunk, and I met my bunkmate, who introduced himself to me as Tennessee. He was a short, soft-spoken man with dark hair and a broad forehead. He, too, was involved in the Dungeons & Dragons game—in fact, he was the dungeon master—and he immediately invited me to join his campaign. Tennesee and I hit it off and spent the rest of the day chatting about elves and dwarves, katanas and broadswords, centaurs and dragons. It was slowly dawning on me that I just might be lucky enough to finish out my remaining three years here, as free from violence and chaos as was possible while a prisoner. I wrote letters to each of my parents, telling them about this positive turn, even though I knew that dad would not respond and mom probably wouldn't either. I didn't care—I had to share some positivity with them.

No sooner had I mailed the letters than things started to turn. Two days after my arrival, I was told to pack up my stuff and move to B dorm. Apparently, they'd made a mistake. I was too dangerous, and my custody level was too high for A dorm, a space for minimum security inmates who were allowed to go outside the prison to work in the fields.

Lucky them.

In B dorm, I was fortunate to be assigned to a bunk way in the back, away from the heat and steam and smell of the bathrooms and showers, away from the noise of the dayroom. My faraway spot also meant that I didn't have to contend with frequent foot traffic past my bunk along with its relentless the stench of unwashed bodies. It never ceased to amaze me how many people did not believe in bathing daily or even weekly, despite running and playing football in the Florida heat day after day. At first, I thought it was a cultural thing, because it seemed like the black inmates were most vocal about it being OK to go days or weeks without bathing, but after a while, I began to realize that it wasn't about race—it was about lack of education. Ignorance comes from that lack, and that lack comes from generational poverty, no place else.

The generational poverty that is prevalent in our nation, predominantly in communities of color, is *the* reason that our prisons are predominantly black, the real reason the prisons foster a culture of ignorance, physical domination, and violence. The inmates most prone to violence were also least likely to bathe regularly and also just happened to be the ones most likely to speak in Ebonics and get offended when someone spoke eloquently or used a word they didn't understand, such as *eloquently*, and can you blame them? They carry a generational burden none of us on the outside can fathom.

The bunk next to me had an inmate named Matthew, a guy with his master's degree in education, tall and lanky with dark hair and glasses taped together at the bridge of his nose. Matthew was incarcerated because he had an inappropriate relationship with one of his students, a child. It was hard for me to admit that because as reprehensible as what Matthew did was, it was also it was really nice to finally have someone intelligent to converse with about topics beyond football, basketball, and fantasy role-playing games. Generally, he didn't talk much. Like most child molesters who get caught, he was immersed in his Bible. So many of them carried the Bible like a shield. As a rule, they'd get job assignments in the chapel for their own protection, and Matthew was no exception. Still, he was kind enough to introduce me to Michael Douglas, the guitar player for the chapel's praise-and-worship band, after I mentioned to him that I missed playing guitar more than nearly any other activity.

Michael was a short, stocky man, dark-skinned and angry. Even when he was sleeping, you could feel the rage roiling off of him, a fury that was prevalent in every movement, every mannerism. I made the effort to connect with him, though, because I, too, knew what it felt like to be angry all the time, to hate everyone around me, to hate the world. Also, I really wanted to play guitar again, and he was my ticket. When I met him, I saw that he was reading an issue of *Guitar Player* magazine.

"Sorry to bother you," I began, "but I saw the picture of John Petrucci on the cover of your magazine. He's my favorite guitarist, though I am not a fan of Dream Theater. Could I look at your mag when you're finished with it?"

"I don't know you," he replied.

"I apologize," I said. "My name's Joshua, I just transferred here. I play guitar too, but I'm not very good. I won't damage your magazine, but I understand if you don't want to let me hold it."

"I'll think about it," he said, shaking the magazine to let me know he was not interested in any further discussion.

In fact, he never did let me read the magazine that day. He looked me in the eye as he put it in his locker, just before we went to chow, almost daring me to say something.

I let it go.

I was on a bigger mission.

I put in a request form to speak to the chaplain, because I was still struggling with the loss of my grandmother. I also wanted to request a conversation with my father, and I needed the chaplain to see my face so that I could ask to play that guitar. Surprisingly, I got called to his office *before* I received a formal response to the request form. Turns out, he was one of the rare, really good-hearted chaplains in the entire state. He responded quickly and took his role of adviser, counselor, and supporter seriously. In fact, he'd been in trouble more than once for caring about inmates enough to do the right thing and advocate for us. He granted me a conversation with my dad on speakerphone, nearly five full minutes!

"Dad, do you remember when I was thirteen, and Bubbe came to visit us in Venice? Do you remember what she said when she walked in and saw the landfill that I called my bedroom?"

"I remember her visiting," my father replied, "but I don't recall what she said to you."

"She said to me, 'Joshua dah-lingk, why is your room so messy, dah-lingk? If your room is messy and full of chaos, dah-lingk, then your mind will be messy and full of chaos, dah-lingk. Joshua, dah-lingk, if your mind is messy and chaotic, then your life will be messy and full of chaos, dah-lingk. You don't want to live like that Joshua, dah-lingk. So clean your room dah-lingk.'"

Before I finished, my voice broke, and Dad and I cried together. This was the first time I had ever heard him cry, and it was profoundly moving.

"She loved you very much," he told me. "You and she had a very special relationship. I never told her you were in prison, just that you were away for work. She was always so very proud of you. You were always her favorite."

"Joshua," the chaplain interrupted. "I'm afraid I can't justify letting you talk on the phone much longer. We'll both get in trouble. Please say your goodbyes."

I said goodbye to my father and told him that I loved him. I was so raw I almost forgot to ask the chaplain about the praise band. As I was walking out of his office, I paused and turned.

"Chap," I began, "I...I forgot to mention. I'm a guitarist. Do you have any room on the praise band for another guitar player?"

"I can have you try out," the chaplain replied. "But you're listed in the computer as Jewish. The praise band is a Christian band. You'd need to submit a change of religion request first."

"Can I do that now?" I said. "I don't really care what the computer has me listed as."

"Sure." He handed me a form. "We'll get you on the callout tomorrow with the rest of the band."

The next day, I was called out for band practice. Michael Douglas was clearly displeased when he left the dorm and I accompanied him. I didn't think I'd done anything to offend him—he was just angry at the world. The guy seemed to hate everyone. I followed him and the other musicians to the chapel, where I was handed a crappy, red electric guitar that had intermittent electronics. I hadn't touched a guitar in roughly two years, and I was never a great guitarist even when I was playing every day. I'd only played for a year, all self-taught, so it was no surprise that I was extremely nervous. To make matters worse, I only knew how to play open cords, and contemporary Christian rock often requires bar chords.

Somehow, I managed to not embarrass myself too badly, and my self-depreciating attitude won over every one of my fellow musicians—except Michael. All three of the singers, the bass player, the keyboard player, and the drummer convinced the chaplain that I was a good fit because I was humble and a quick learner. Besides, they needed an additional guitarist to play rhythm.

Day after day, my name appeared on the daily callout sheet for band practice or for various Christian services that we played. One thing I had to admit: Michael Douglas was a phenomenal guitar player. I never met anyone else who could play a note-perfect rendition of Jimi's "All Along the Watchtower." Michael insisted that I learn how to play bar chords, even though my pinky finger didn't want to cooperate at first. My stage fright went away quickly, too, and soon enough, band practice became the brightest part of my day. The chaplain treated us like actual people, joking with us and calling us by our first names. Whatever we asked of him, he tried to do.

I was in constant pain every day, so when I wasn't in the chapel playing guitar, I was doing yoga to keep some of the pain at bay.

Every place I'd been in the Florida Department of Corrections had a thriving black market, particularly when it came to drugs. The two most common items were tobacco and spice. Spice was also called K2 or incense, the synthetic marijuana sold in convenience stores that was really just tobacco or incense sprayed with roach killer. Spice has the most disgusting stench—and powerful hallucinogenic properties. It seemed like everyone who smoked it either saw the devil, had a seizure, got fucked up like nothing I'd ever seen before, or all of the above. Most people called it "tweaking out," and watching someone tweak out was usually annoying, sometimes scary, and on rare occasions incredibly entertaining.

One particular afternoon, there was nothing going on in the chapel, nothing going on anywhere on the compound, and we were all confined to the dormitory. Matthew and I were sitting on the floor between our bunks with our backs against the wall, having a deep, philosophical conversation about the Bible and history. Suddenly, there was a commotion on the opposite side of the dorm in the front left corner. Two guys who were sitting there smoking got in some sort of altercation. One guy got up, swaying like he was drunk. He mumbled something incoherent and threw the most slow-motion punch I'd ever seen at his friend. His friend ducked, also in slow motion, and ended up sitting on his bunk. Then the first inmate started running around the dorm while taking his clothes off.

"I'm hot," he said. "I'm so hot. It's too hot in here!"

By the time he crossed the dorm and got to where we were, he was completely naked. About ten feet in front of us, an inmate was lying on his bunk, reading a book. The naked man grabbed a bottle of water from someone, then jumped up onto the edge of the bunk. He squatted down, with his genitals right in the face of the guy reading the book. The guy reading the book scooted over to the other side of the bunk and got up, while the naked inmate laid down on this bunk and held the water bottle against his dick, still muttering, "So hot! So hot in here!"

Matthew and I looked at each other, stunned speechless. I think somebody went to the officer station and snitched, because two overweight, country-bumpkin officers came into the dorm and ordered the inmate to get up and get dressed.

"No!" he shouted as he jumped up and ran toward the bathroom. All of the hand sinks were located on an island that was about five feet tall with a flat-tiled top. He ran, climbed up on a sink, and then stretched out on top of the island with both hands out to his sides like Spider-Man hiding against a wall, butt naked with a raging erection like a flagpole.

"No!" he shouted. "You can't see me! I'm invisible! You can't see me!"

The officers attempted to grab his legs and arms, but he was kicking and flailing each time they tried to grab him. One of the officers got a blanket and threw the blanket over him while the other officer grabbed his ankles. They pulled him down and rolled him inside of the blanket, and then they carried him out under their arms like an old rug.

"Did you see that?" Matthew turned to me. "Or did I just imagine a naked black man squatting on another man's face before being carried out in a rolled blanket?"

"I am pretty sure we both just shared the same hallucination," I replied. "There is no way that really just happened."

"We are going to get shook down," Matthew says. "Hard."

"No doubt."

Sure enough, the next day, when we were supposed to be released for callouts, the loudspeakers blasted, "Everyone, on your bunks! Everyone on your bunks!" Fifteen officers came storming into the dorm, nasty and aggressive. They started ripping sheets and blankets off of everyone's bunks, cutting open mattresses and pillowcases with pocket knives, pulling out the stuffing. They opened lockers and dumped everyone's belongings into piles on the floor—bad news because everyone's stuff getting mixed together meant there were going to be some fights. After about an hour, they had finished ransacking the entire dormitory. A few inmates were escorted out in handcuffs for possession of tobacco, spice, and cell phones. One inmate was escorted out for having pornography, yet the pornography itself was given to another inmate rather than confiscated.

Huh?

Didn't make any sense, but then, nothing here ever did.

As we were all putting our bunks and belongings back together, like hurricane survivors trying to sort through the wreckage of our homes, Michael tossed the *Guitar Player* magazine on my bunk and said, "You can read it now. I'm done with it."

AUGUST 2015

"Bork!" an officer shouted. "Come get your mail!"

That alone shocked me because, as a rule, I did not get mail, and it was not for lack of trying. I sent out at least four letters per week, and I mean every week—two to Maddie, one to my father, and one to my mother—but the most response I got was *maybe* a letter from my mother twice per year if I was lucky, nothing from Maddie ever, and the single letter from my dad was when Bubbe passed away.

Who could it possibly be from?

I walked up to the officer's station, sure that I was being set up for some kind of a prank. Or maybe it was something to do with the request form I sent out six months prior. I showed the officer my ID badge and she passed me an envelope through the slot.

It was another letter from my father.

My heart sunk. I couldn't handle another crisis or death, couldn't even open the thing. I walked back to my bunk and tossed it on my pillow and went back to reading the latest *Guitar Player* magazine.

"Aren't you going to read your mail?" Matthew asked me.

"No," I said. "I can't do it. I know it's something unpleasant. Would you read it and tell me...but only if it's something...OK."

"Sure." Matthew got off his bunk and picked up my mail. After a few moments, he looked up. "Your dad wants to come visit you before the end of September."

I snatched the letter out of his hand and started reading it myself.

> *Joshua,*
>
> *I'm sorry that I haven't responded to your letters. I haven't known what to say. I've started writing you so many times, but never sent any of them. I want to come visit you in the next two weeks, because I'm going to be gone for a while. Please let me know what I need to do to see you.*
>
> *Love, Dad*

I ran to the phone, and I called him. He didn't answer, so I tried again. No answer. I called a third time. When he didn't answer the third time, I ran back to my bunk, and I started writing him a letter.

> *Dad,*
>
> *I got your letter. I really want to see you too. They won't let you come see me unless you fill out a visitation application and get it approved. I'm including one with this letter. Please fill*

it out and send it back to me as soon as possible. I hope that
they approve it in time for you to come see me before you leave.

Love, Josh

In a frenzy, I scrambled to get my hands on a visitor application. I
was terrified that they wouldn't approve it in time. I got everything
together and dropped it in the mail slot. I kept getting in line for the
phone, kept trying until finally he answered.

A robot voice said: "Thank you for using T-Netix. You may start
your conversation now."

"Hello?" My father's voice was clear in my ear.

"Dad, I got your letter. I sent you the form you need to fill out,
but I don't know if it'll get to you in time. Please go online to the
DOC website and print the visitor application form. Send it back to
me like a normal letter. Otherwise, classification will intercept it and
take their own sweet time about processing the application. I really
want to see you."

"I really want to see you too," he replied. "I will do that this
evening. Please let me know as soon as it gets approved. I'll come
right away."

"I will, Dad," I whispered, tears filling up my eyes. "I will."

About two weeks later, I got notification from the classification
office that my father had been approved for a visit. Once again, I
called over and over again until he answered, and I let him know that
he could come see me. He told me that he'd come up right away, the
very next weekend. I couldn't contain my joy. I told everyone who'd
listen. I knew I was annoying the hell out of everyone. Couldn't
help it.

Saturday afternoon my name was called. I was so excited I was
practically teleporting, floating over the ground. When I got to visitation, I was strip-searched before I was allowed to enter the visiting

area. I was so excited I didn't even care about the indignity of having to get naked, bend over, and spread my ass cheeks. I got back into clothes, pulled on my shoes, and walked into visitation.

I almost didn't recognize my own father.

"Dad!" I said. "Where are your glasses?"

My father had worn gigantic trifocals my entire life. He was blind as a bat without them.

"Eh," Dad said, shrugging, "I did the LASIK."

I was not allowed to run, but I walked fast as I could and threw my arms around him as soon as I was close enough to do so, hugged him as tight as I could. I wanted this hug to be laser-etched in my mind. I needed it to be.

"That's enough, inmate!" an officer barked. "No touching!"

I reluctantly let go of my father, and we sat at the table side by side.

"Other side of the table," the same officer barked. "No touching, hands where we can see them."

I complied, getting up and moving to the other side.

"I'm so happy to see you, Dad. I don't have the words."

He nodded knowingly.

"Not that it matters but…why…why now? I mean, after all this time?"

"Josh," Dad began, "I wanted to have this conversation in person. I have cancer."

My stomach dropped as I hazed over—I heard the rest of my father's words as though from a great distance,

"I have tumors on my kidneys. It is an incredibly rare cancer, and there are only five doctors in the world who are willing to risk operating. I wanted to see you before I have the surgery, in case I don't make it."

"Dad—"

"Joselyn and I have done a lot of research. I'm going to the best doctor in the world for this procedure. But…it is extremely risky, and I may lose my kidneys or die. I am scared."

I'm ashamed to admit that an anger flared up in me. He'd ignored me for over two years, then reached out to me to tell me that my bubbe died, went back to ignoring me, then came to see me just to say goodbye? I felt rejected in a way a civilian probably can't imagine, but the deeper truth was I was scared. This was the first time my father had ever admitted to me that he was scared of *anything*. In fact, I don't know what scared me worse—the thought that I might lose him in two weeks or the strange realization that he was mostly here because he wanted to make sure he didn't die with his son hating him. In that moment, it didn't feel like he was there to see me at all. He was here for himself, for his guilt.

The anger surged, but it also snapped me back to reality, broke me free from the shock of the news, back to the daily numbness I lived with just to survive. And strangely enough, this numbness made it just a little easier to interact with him.

We got to talk for about thirty minutes before the officer told me it was time to go. Thirty minutes. My dad had arrived before 7:00 a.m. and didn't get to see me until just before three in the afternoon. Then thirty minutes later—the end?

At this point, I didn't care what the officer said.

If this was the last time I could ever hug my father, I was going to hug him. If the officers decided to beat me for it, so be it. I could endure a beating. I'd already proven that a dozen times over. If they threw me in solitary confinement again, so be it.

This was the man I had spent my life trying to make proud. And knowing that this might be the last time he'd see me—in here, the worst of all possible outcomes—I didn't want to let him go.

I hugged my father so hard that I heard his bones creak. The officer was telling me to let go and move away, but I kept on ignoring him. In a very real way, I was holding on to my father for dear life—my life and his. I wouldn't let go, *couldn't* let go, and if I did, I might never see him again.

Finally, the officers grabbed my arms, pried me away. I flared up, ready to kill them for this, for taking this last hug away.

"Josh," my father said solemnly, "*don't*. It's going to be OK."

I went limp, and I apologized to the officers.

"I haven't seen my father in years," I mumbled, "and I just found out he has cancer." I was still mumbling as they led me out of the visitation room.

When I got back to the dorm, I started filling out request forms to the chaplain, medical, and classification. My father might need a kidney, and I would be damned if I let him go without a fight. If need be, I'd give him one of mine. The Department of Corrections couldn't condemn him to death if he needed a kidney and I was a match, could they? *He* had committed no crime.

For the next few weeks, I sent requests every single day, and for every single request, I received a response from medical: "Denied. We do not allow inmates to donate organs as we will not pay for your recovery."

So, I asked, if my family paid for the recovery, I *might* get permission?

"Denied."

But I wasn't giving up.

I started writing letters to the state, to the warden, to classification, to the assistant warden, to the colonel in charge of security. I could not let my father go, not without a fight. Eventually, I was called into the office of the captain, and I was told in clear terms that I was to stop all efforts to be approved for donating my kidney. The captain told me that if I failed to comply, I would be put in confinement for "abuse of the grievance process."

The next day, I submitted a request form asking to be transferred to a facility closer to home—I had discovered an obscure provision of Florida law regarding inmates reentering into society and the undue burden being so far from home places upon both the inmate and their family. Obviously, proximity is necessary for successful reintegration without recidivism, specifically, less than a hundred miles. If I couldn't get them to let me do the right thing, then I was going to do everything in my power to get transferred somewhere else where *somebody* might listen.

One particular sunny day about a month after I was transferred from the main unit, I saw a familiar face exiting the chow hall.

"Trevor!" I shouted. "How are you, man!"

Trevor jumped in surprise, and his face lit up with a huge smile.

"Josh!" he said. "I'm really glad to see a friendly face. I just got transferred over here yesterday, and I'm not sure how I feel about it. I had a good thing going at the main unit."

"It's not so bad here," I replied. "Just give it a few days. You should come check out the chapel; there's a great praise-and-worship band here. I play guitar!"

"I don't know about all that," he said, "but the food in the chow hall is certainly not the exquisite delicacies I'm accustomed to at the main unit."

"Yeah, I know," I said, "and the accommodations suck. But I think you'll find there's a little more freedom and lot less violence here."

Suddenly, Sergeant Godzilla started yelling at us to disperse. I didn't call her Sergeant Godzilla just because she was a big woman with the nastiest scowl and demeanor of any person I had ever met in my life. I called her that because her hair was plastered with so much gel, hairspray and glue that she seemed to be wearing armor. That hair wouldn't move in a hurricane.

"I gotta go," I said.

"Peace out, man."

Of everyone I met while incarcerated, Trevor was by far the most educated and intelligent, but there were others. There was Joshua Hagen—they called him Muslim Josh and called me Jew Josh to differentiate. But Hagen was a white guy, and he was absolutely bonkers, convinced that the government was out to get him because he was a political dissident, having been accused of "kidnapping" his own kids with his wife and fleeing to Cuba. He was incredibly intelligent too, and a great conversationalist, if you could keep the talk away from anything that gave him an opening to start up his conspiracy theories. He was an aeronautical engineer, his father was an engineer, and his wife was an engineer. Matthew, him, and I ate in the chow hall together on a regular basis, but as smart as he was, I never *really* connected with him, not like with Trevor. Trevor had a certain charisma, and as soon as he came to the work camp, our friendship really grew.

One particular evening in August, as we were standing in line at the chow hall waiting to go in, Trevor looked over my shoulder and said, "I see that old man every day, just chugging along. Every time I see him, that song by Cake jumps into my head."

"What song?"

Trevor started singing quietly, and everything around me faded away except the old man and his walker, as if I was looking at him from the opposite end of a tunnel with the sun setting behind him, a song about a old race car driver, chugging away, leaving his girl to be lonely, and heartbroken, driving into the sunset and abandoning all else.

I saw it, and I understood: the old man with his walker, determinedly chugging along. Even though he was moving at a snail's pace, his chin and bottom lip jutted out, head and neck extended forward. He was in a race.

Trevor kept singing.

Day after day, I played in the chapel band and spent most of my free time writing letters to Madeline, to my father, and to my mother. Occasionally, every six months or so, I got a letter from Beverly Dickinson, Mark Dickinson's mother. It was so sweet of her to reach out, but also crushing that the eighty-five-year-old mother of an inmate that I'd met in my first days in prison and only interacted with for about six weeks cared more about me than my own mother and father.

There was another upside to being at this compound: one of the dayshift officers just happened to be a young man that I'd taught when I was working with the military units. With his support, I was allowed to teach tai chi out on the rec yard as a way to generate currency. Anywhere else, teaching tai chi or yoga would have been strictly prohibited. Insane as it sounds, they were considered martial arts skills that could potentially empower inmates to overthrow the guards. Even here, I could only teach tai chi on days when this particular officer, a mere boy of nineteen or so, was on duty.

Mostly, I taught Muslim Josh because Trevor wasn't interested and Michael was too volatile. I didn't like the idea of teaching a rage-filled, rock-hard body builder. On the days I couldn't teach, I was forced to mingle. Mostly, I wandered aimlessly. After a few weeks of feeling all out of sorts on the sidelines, I decided that I was going to man up and approach the three guys tossing a Frisbee around. One of them was Robert, the keys player in the praise band.

"Hey, guys," I said. "Mind if I join you?"

"Not at all," replied the first, an older man with a cane who I didn't know and hadn't seen before.

I tossed the Frisbee around with them a few times, but it was boring, worse than wandering around aimlessly.

"Have you guys ever played ultimate Frisbee?" I asked.

"No," they both replied. "What is it?"

"OK," I began. "It is like a combination of football, soccer, basketball, and Frisbee. You have end zones and touchdowns like football, and a throw off like the kickoff. Like basketball, it is no contact, and you cannot travel with the Frisbee—it must be thrown to move. Like soccer, you have to work together and pass it back and forth until you get to the other end. If you drop it or it gets intercepted, it gets turned over to the other team like in basketball. It's really intense and really fun."

"There are only four of us," Robert said. "Can we play with only four?"

"Absolutely!" I replied. "We can play two on two, and I bet other people will see us, get curious, and want to join."

We broke into two separate teams and walked to opposite ends of the soccer field. We started playing, and I was immediately reminded of my injured back and knees. I was not up to running, and every step was agony, lightning shooting from my low back down to my feet, but I pushed through it. Also, I couldn't afford to show weakness, because then I would be forced to fight for no reason other than being a white guy in pain, like a wounded gazelle surrounded by hungry hyenas. Starting up the game was clearly a mistake, but it was too late to turn back.

As we played, an older man known as "Kick" (because he had been a professional kickboxer prior to his incarceration) saw us and decided to give it a shot. Within a few minutes, Michael joined in, and we were up to three on three—now things got more intense. Michael's anger and aggression emanated out of him like a pulsing supernova, visible in his every move, explosive throws and aggressive blocking. His intensity forced everyone else to kick it up from a casual game to an all-out Super Bowl competition.

Before too long, the intensity of our game caught the attention of others on the rec yard. Usually, the Hispanic inmates stuck to dominoes and soccer, the black guys stuck to basketball and football.

Even the white supremacists had their zone—the pull-up bar and dip bar. Not anymore. Within four days, we had *forty* people playing every single day. The entire football field and soccer field had been converted to an ultimate Frisbee field. Our games were so intense that the officers started coming to watch.

Here's how it works: With ultimate Frisbee, newcomers often start by trying to play like they're in a game of standard football, but all quickly realize that this game is *way* more fast-paced, like a speed game of backyard ball, with the Frisbee getting passed back and forth so rapidly that it'd make your head spin. Many of us didn't have shoes. We were each given a pair of foam Crocs and forced to wear them until there were holes in the bottom. Your feet would bleed, and it was nearly impossible to get a new pair. Out there on the field, half the players did it barefoot!

When we hit the weekend, the number of participants nearly doubled. Everybody who had job assignments throughout the week jumped in the game on Saturdays and Sundays. We were playing thirty against thirty, and it was glorious chaos. Every time we played, I was amazed that nobody got injured, and nobody fought. At football games and at least half the basketball games, there would *always* be a fight. Not here.

As it was late summer in Florida, hurricane season was upon us, with serious winds due to a large tropical storm nearby. Every time we threw the Frisbee, the wind grabbed it, yanked it fifty feet up in the air, and then spun it in the exact opposite direction that anyone intended for it to go. Still, we played on.

For many participants, ultimate Frisbee was the only thing they looked forward to, and the only thing that brought them joy. I personally witnessed the number of fights and even the general hostility on the compound dropping—and the officers and many other inmates saw it too. When you're having so much fun and burning so many calories, there's just nothing left for anger or violence.

"Hey, guys," I said, midsummer, "do you think we can get our hands on the football? We can play the exact same game, using a football instead of a Frisbee, and then the wind won't be an issue."

"Yo, Bork! I gotchu. Heads up!"

I turned around in the direction of the voice just in time to get hit square in the face with a football. My head snapped back as the football ricocheted straight up, and I fell to the ground as the football came back down and landed on my face *again*.

"Thanks, dipshit!" I shouted, getting up.

We started playing the same game of ultimate Frisbee using a football, and the intensity got kicked up even further. All of the people who were phenomenal athletes and football players but who couldn't throw a Frisbee for shit were suddenly *superstars*. Now we had guys that were throwing hundred-yard passes as the game went into full swing. One of the fastest runners on the entire compound was a little white boy with platinum-blond hair that everyone called Powder. As soon as he saw a football getting thrown, he decided that the game was worth participating in. Even in foam Crocs, he was faster than anyone else on the compound, whether they were wearing shoes or running barefoot. He threw a perfect spiral for a hundred yards every time, and he was like four and a half feet tall. He was a cocky little son of a bitch, but damn, if you didn't want him on your team,

In September 2015, I heard my name called, and I was told to "roll it up." Once again, I was being transferred. I had mixed feelings about this. I really didn't want to start all over again, to have to fight, prove myself, learn every new officer's pet peeves, discover who I could trust, who was a shark, and so forth. With every move, you had to create a whole new routine. Still, I had not lost the dream of getting approval to give my dad my kidney.

My dad was a jerk, a know-it-all who was rarely there when I needed him and always quick to point out how he had helped me when it was convenient for him, but he was *my* dad, *my* jerk of a father, and more than a few times, he really *did* know it all, and I believed that he did love me in his own way. In a way, he was all I had. Giving him an organ with nothing to fear but ibuprofen for five days postoperation in a filthy cesspool of disease and bacteria, well, even if it killed me to save him, it was worth it somehow. My dad was the only person in my life who had never lied to me, not even a small white lie. He was also the only person who never used love as a tool to manipulate or coerce.

Dad had a lot of flaws, and was not always the best dad, but he always wanted what was best for me, and he never expected more out of me than I was capable of. Everyone else saw something in me, most called it "potential" but whatever it was, it was held over my head like "yeah, we know you are four years old and haven't learned multiplication, but you have potential so we expect a perfect score on this advanced calculus exam." My sisters would get rewarded if they brought home Cs in school because my mom was so proud they had passed, but if I brought home a 99 percent on any assignment, I would be grounded because I had the "potential" to be perfect at everything.

Dad? Dad was proud of me for doing my best, regardless of the outcome. I won second place at my first-ever fencing tournament. Dad acted like I'd won an Olympic gold; he was so proud. I participated in a ROTC competition and didn't win anything. Dad was just as proud for that, because I'd given it everything I had. There was no one else in my life who had never betrayed my trust, always told me the truth as if I was an adult even when I was a child, and no one else who was proud of me for doing my best when my best wasn't perfect. My dad was my best friend for most of my life. Everyone in the grocery store knew us because we always walked in with our arms around the other's shoulders. We'd done everything together for years. Despite our differences, there was no one on earth other than my father who had ever earned my trust, and there was no one else on earth who had loved me unconditionally.

As I packed up my meager possessions, I was approached by Michael.

"Hey, man," he began. "Good luck. Keep your head down, don't get angry, and get on the praise band wherever you go. You're gonna be all right. And I'm going to miss you."

He held out his hand, we shook, and it was a heartbreaker. This was so out of character for Michael, with his armor of nonstop rage and aggression. I pulled him in and gave him a tight hug. He stiffened for a moment, then hugged me back.

POLK—CHAPEL BANDS
AND CHILD MOLESTERS

I arrived at Polk Correctional Institution at the end of September. It was hot, there was no breeze, and the whole compound sweltered like a wet blanket pressing down upon me. The place was, once again, incredibly unusual, but I was getting used to it.

The first thing I noticed was that inmates were moving around leisurely, unsupervised. Up till this point, everywhere I'd been, our movement was controlled. Every hour on the hour, guards would unlock and open the gates for five minutes and allow movement—that is, if you could justify that you were authorized to be moving around the compound. Here there were no fences and no gates outside the

ones around the perimeter. Inmates appeared to come and go as they
pleased. The chow hall, chapel, and visitation park were located in
a central area, and the compound itself was shaped like a dog bone,
with three dorms on either end, and a long stretch of sidewalk and
road in between. Plus, there was a rec yard on either end of the compound! And flowers! And inmates sitting under trees!

What was this—summer camp?

After being processed, I found myself in alpha dorm. The inmates there did not seem happy to see me. After eavesdropping a
little, I realized that this was the so-called faith-based dorm only for
those participating in Christian programs. Their schedules were dominated with one religious class after another. What this *also* meant was
that this was the snitch dorm, where everybody came to stay safe and
be protected while they ratted each other out in an effort to preserve
the perfect Beverly-Hills-in-prison environment. Also, this is where
all the child molesters and crybabies came, because they, too, were
protected here.

As soon as I figured that out, I didn't want to be in this dorm
any more than they wanted me here.

I didn't want to hear grown men talking about children in a
sexual way like it was normal. And prison was hard enough without
having to run to the officers like a Karen over every perceived slight.
Deep down, I knew I was going to have to hurt someone in order to
get moved out of this dorm. On the bright side, at least I could feel
guilt-free about hurting a baby rapist.

I received my callout to go to classification and be assigned a
job. I wandered across the compound leisurely, enjoying this incredible sense of freedom. Not being manhandled and herded like cattle
was liberating—more than a civilian can imagine. When I arrived at
classification, there were thirty or so inmates milling around waiting—and it was more craziness. Everywhere else, we'd be forced into
orderly lines, facing front, silent, with three or more thugs in uni-

forms looking for a reason to abuse us. Then, after about forty minutes, some civilians would come out looking very angry and hostile,
like they had somewhere better to be, and made it clear that they
hated us and did not consider us human. Here, they just called your
name, and you entered the building, one at a time—hit by the bliss-
fully cold AC. When they called for me, I decided to move in slow
motion to drag this out as long as I could.

Seriously, folks, one of the most undervalued aspects of civiliza-
tion is air-conditioning. When you spend your days in an unventilat-
ed cement box with heat and humidity so intense the walls actually
sweat, when you spend your only outdoor time in 103-degree heat
and direct sunlight, with temperatures so oppressive that grown men
attempt suicide just to get into an air conditioned hospital room for
twenty-four hours, you realize just what air-conditioning is worth.

It's a transcendent bliss, a divine rapture that envelops your soul.

Once in classification, I was asked the same stupid questions
I've been asked at every compound upon arrival: "Do you have a high
school diploma?"

Uh yeah, dumbass. It says so on your screen. You're only asking
me because if I tell you anything other than what's on your screen,
you'll throw me in confinement for lying to an officer and push my
release date further into the future, you fucking scumbag.

"Yes, ma'am," I said.

"Do you enjoy hospitality and food service?"

No, not at all. I hated working in the kitchen, watching grown
men have sex with squash and then serving it to other grown men.

"No, ma'am"

"Do you like landscaping?"

No, sorry, I do not like performing free slave labor, mowing
your grass with a push lawnmower and pulling weeds in a prison,
especially when I can't take a shower afterward.

"No, ma'am."

"Do you have a background as a lawyer or a paralegal?"

"No, I do not," I said. "I can, however, touch-type sixty words per minute without looking at the keyboard. Don't know if that matters."

But of course, I know it matters. They'll put me in the air-conditioned law library as a typist if there's an opening. Sweet gig, good dough.

"Do you like cleaning?"

Of course not. I'm not a maid or mommy. Come to think of it, I do not have any desire to clean up after a bunch of dirty grown men, washing their shower stalls, toilets, sinks, or sweeping their floors with all their pubic hairs and dingleberries.

"No, ma'am."

"Do you like folding laundry?"

Well, strange as it may seem, I have zero desire to handle dirty undergarments from a bunch of nasty men who can't properly bath, wear two pairs of skid-marked boxers for seven days with only one pair getting washed every three days.

"No, ma'am."

"Are you interested in teaching other inmates?"

Teaching a bunch of high school or middle school dropouts who do not want to be learning? Where being their teacher only makes me a target of their scorn because they feel disrespected when they don't understand my vocabulary or struggle with a basic concept like putting a period at the end of sentences? Nope. I guess not. No desire to get jumped again for trying to speak to someone like they might actually be intelligent.

"No, ma'am," I replied. "I came to prison alone, and I will leave alone. I am only interested in things that will better my chances for success upon being released. I will never see anyone here again and couldn't care less if they want to learn or not."

Am I interested in learning a trade or vocation?

Not really. Plus, it didn't turn out so good for me last time. I have no desire to work with my hands as a mechanic and less desire to learn computer programming. Plumbing? Gross.

"Yes, ma'am," I said, surprising myself. "Plumbing would probably be the one I am the most interested in. I can learn auto mechanics on YouTube, and I know I have no interest in computers because that's what my father does, and it has always been boring to me. Plumbing, though, well, at the least it'll make me a better homeowner, a better husband and father, even though I don't intend to do this as a profession."

Am I interested in fitness and health?

"Yes, ma'am." I sat a little straighter in my seat. "As you can see, I was a rec orderly at ACI before being transferred. That would be my ideal job assignment. If it would be possible to assign me there, I would really appreciate it."

Still, it didn't matter. However they scored these questions, I found myself assigned to the plumbing-and-pipe-trade program. Wonderful. I was going to be cleaning toilets for a bunch of filthy inmates who ate garbage prison food and did massive amounts of illicit drugs (which, for the record, makes for horrible bowel movements and urine so putrid, so toxic it smells radioactive.) I came to prison completely disease-free but now was probably going to leave with hepatitis, HIV, SARS, SIDS, rabies, herpes, scabies, Ebola, E. coli, and salmonella. Fan-fucking-tastic.

Like any sane person would, I arrived to my job assignment expecting the worst, and I was not disappointed. The classroom was a warehouse bay with no air-conditioning and no fans, row after row of old-fashioned desks, and piles of pipes and fittings in various stages of decay scattered around the room covered in cobwebs. There was also a mini mock-up of a kitchen and of a bathroom, and some old water heaters in one corner. There was also a smaller classroom off to one side, next to the instructor's office. All of the inmates immediately sat down, opened textbooks, and started reading.

What the heck? Who does that? Even when I was in school, nobody just sat down, opened his or her book, and started reading. What kind of hell did I just land in? Where was the class clown? Where was the teacher's pet? Used to be, I was always bullied and picked on for being the only person so hyperfocused on learning, the one who sat down and started right away.

The teacher assigned me a book and told me to start reading. When I finished the chapter, I was to do the problems in the back and turn them in. But learning a trade from a textbook didn't feel right. I read through the chapter in about ten minutes and took the test. When I handed it in to the teacher, he told me scornfully, "There's no way you finished the first chapter and took the test that fast. You must have cheated. I do not tolerate cheating!"

"No, sir," I told him. "I'm just a fast reader with a photographic memory. If you want me to take the test again, I'd be happy to do so."

"Yes," he said. "That way I can send you to confinement for cheating and lying."

I took the test again in front of him, in about five minutes this time. I scored a perfect one hundred, with him breathing his disgusting breath in my ear. Toothpaste isn't that expensive, dude.

"See?" I said. "I didn't cheat either time. This material is a no-brainer: Identify a screwdriver. Identify an extension cord. Can you please allow me to learn at my own pace? I'll finish all four years of the material in a couple of weeks and be out of your hair."

"You can learn the material and take the tests as fast as you want, but I cannot enter more than one per week," he said, "sometimes less. Each module, each chapter and test, have a specific number of hours that you are supposed to devote to learning the material, and I cannot enter anything faster than that regarding completion. But I can mark you as present and participating once you finish everything, and you can go to the canteen or rec yard instead of coming here."

"Deal."

Within five weeks, I had completed three and a half years of the material and vocational training, passed all the tests, and turned in *everything*. I had only been slowed by the lockdowns that occurred every few days when the B-shift officers worked, because they didn't want to do anything so they just left us confined to our tiny cells all day and blamed it on "security issues." What difference did it make? This so-called teacher was not a plumber and couldn't answer any questions I had about plumbing, beyond what he could find in his answer key in the teacher's edition of the book. In fact, he was a retired psychologist who'd quit the mental health profession because it was too painful for him. Strange, then, that he thought working in a prison was somehow going to be less traumatizing. Sure enough, before the semester was over, he had a mental breakdown and was hospitalized. Next day, the plumbing program was shut down.

* * *

One of the first things that I did upon my arrival at Polk was make an appointment with the chaplain to try out for the praise-and-worship band. Chaplain Ortega was the head chaplain there, and from what I heard, he was a hardcore Apostolic Pentecostal, born-again Christian who liked a lively worship service. Like with screaming and spittle flying everywhere, people pretending to have a spirit overtake them while they lay on the ground twitching and speaking gibberish. While I was meeting with Chaplain Ortega, I could hear the band practicing in the main sanctuary.

"*Ever eeee thingggg,*" I heard booming from the other room. "*You're everything to me!*"

"So," Chaplain Ortega was saying, "you want to play in the band. Do you have any experience?"

"Yes, sir. I've been playing with the praise-and-worship band at ACI for the past six months."

"Are you a Christian?" Chaplain Ortega asked.

"I believe in the God of Abraham, Isaac, and Joseph, yes." I said.

"Good," Chaplain Ortega said, as if that settled it. "Go see Marcus Sumes. He'll get you a guitar, and you can try out to play with Destiny."

"Thank you, Chap.," I replied as I got up to leave. "I won't let you down."

I walked out of his office, and as I turned the corner and opened the door to the sanctuary, my ears were assaulted by sounds of Southern gospel, with undertones of jazz keyboard, played at a volume far greater than the limited space required. Entering the main sanctuary from a door at the front to the right of the stage, I saw the mostly empty pews facing me. As I looked to my right, I saw a stage with two separate sets of keyboards in the center, an amp and guitar stands, drums on the opposite side, an amp and guitar stand next to the drums, and a bass amp and guitar stand directly in front of the drums. At floor level in front of the stage, there were five mic stands. There were men standing at each mic, a man seated at each set of keyboards, a man seated at the drums, and men standing at each amp. I sat at the pew to the front and waited until they finish their song, then I spoke up.

"Hi, I'm supposed to speak to Sumes about trying out for rhythm guitar," I said.

A young, slender black man with small, round glasses seated at the center set of keyboards looked up at me and said, "I'm Sumes. Grab a guitar and show me what you can do."

Looking around, confused as to where I was supposed to get a guitar, I heard Marcus speak into the mic. "Give him your guitar for a moment."

The only white guy in the band, an older hard-ass white supremacist, gave Marcus a dirty look but lifted the guitar over his head and held it out to me.

I took the guitar and started playing "Under the Bridge" by the Red Hot Chili Peppers. Marcus stopped me and asked, "Can you play an F-sharp seven flat nine, followed by a C major nine add four add 6 flat thirteen flat five?"

"I'm sorry," I responded. "Can you please speak English?"

Marcus played a chord on piano using all ten fingers, his foot, and seven fingers from two other people's hands, then used his other foot and three more hands from the drummer and the bass player.

"This chord, followed by this chord—can you play these chords?"

"I only have six strings, and four fingers with which to play them," I said. "But I can play an F sharp and a C major." I did, and it sounded like shit because I was nervous.

"Good," Marcus said. "Now lift your pinky like so and that makes it the seven."

I still had no idea what he was talking about, but I lifted my pinky and got a rich sound with more body, more jazz and flavor than before—really nice. I didn't know that simply lifting my pinky could get that much more character out of a chord, and I was impressed.

"If you can show me the chords you want, I can copy them till I know what they're called."

The bass player and the drummer started cleaning up, wrapping up cables and putting away equipment.

"I like your attitude," Marcus said. "We can teach you the theory and the chords, but too many guitarists come in here with a need to be a rock star, and that is not the right reason to be playing here."

"I just want to make music," I replied. "Music is where I am happy, where I experience peace. To me, it's the language of love, it's divine. Music transcends all language barriers, and it's the purest form of communication. One of my favorite quotes comes from Bob Marley: 'One good thing about music, when it hits you, you feel no pain.'"

"I am going to give you a shot," Marcus said to me as he started unplugging keyboards. "I like your attitude. I will make sure that the chaplain has your name on the callouts for band practice. If you don't see your name, come anyways. We practice Wednesday afternoon and Saturday morning."

As I left, I was feeling pretty hopeful that the rest of my time might not be so terrible. Playing in the band again, being in school during the day, freedom of movement around the compound, lots of sports and activities to keep me busy—who knows? Maybe the time would start flying by again. If I could find a Dungeons & Dragons game too, things just might be all right.

By the end of my first band practice, I realized I was way out of my depth. Every musician in the band had decades of musical experience, college degrees in music, and spoke a whole different language. I had never before realized that music was a language with its own vocabulary and alphabet, but I learned four years of college-level music theory just in my first two hours of practicing.

Marcus Sumes, the keys player and lead singer, had a degree in music theory and composition, along with thirty years of playing organ and piano in the church as well as a decade of being a professional full-time musician. Apparently, he was called "the packing preacher," because he would go to church every Sunday and play organ with a pistol in his waistband.

John Trueblood, drummer and band leader, was a Vietnam veteran who played in the drumline in college before serving in the army. He was a lifer, was never going to see freedom—sentenced in

1983 for two counts of sexual battery with a weapon or force, also known as rape. I did not find this out until after my release, years later. The band and the music were his only lifelines.

Gene was the bass player. He was a quiet man, tall and lean, in his seventies, though he looked like he was forty. He also had a life sentence, but I never found out why. He moved slowly, didn't say much, and was also very reserved when playing. But I soon learned he was a master. He could really get down, like Flea from the Red Hot Chili Peppers. Unfortunately, he had had a band leader for years who discouraged any type of experimentation or showing off, but give him a bass solo and coax him out of his shell and watch out. The man could play some funk.

Dexter was the other keys player, the only person in the band with no formal musical education, but he was a gifted pianist who could play by feel and sound like Mozart with soul, as long as we stayed in the key of C. Dexter was only a few months away from going home.

Johnny was the lead guitarist. He had a chip on his shoulder, like he was the best guitar player in the world. Actually, he wasn't very good—mostly he played three or four notes over and over when he actually played at all. He frequently turned off his volume because he had stage fright and no real confidence. He was not a lifer, but he had at least fifteen more years to go and had been locked up for a decade or more, for a series of violent crimes. It was strange that someone so shy could also be so egotistical and also be a dangerous criminal all in one.

There were four singers. The first was Marcos Fuentes, a short older Hispanic man who could not carry a tune to save his life but gave it all the heart and soul he had. Sometimes, sound man Johnny Cardona would just turned him off and let howl. Then there was E, a scruffy-looking guy with sleepy eyes who could sing great *some-times*. Dexter took the mic when he wasn't playing keys (and sometimes when he was), and last there was Elliot, a young, baby-faced, soft-spoken guy who could really sing.

I practiced with them twice—just twice!—and then it was showtime. There were chapel services that had a praise-and-worship portion six days per week. Every evening and Saturdays, I headed to the chapel to play a set of songs. We were loud. I loved the blues-and-jazz vibe. I was genuinely happy in those few moments up on stage. The world around me faded away, and all that was left was music. Unfortunately, I also had to sit through the religious service. Sometimes it was not terrible, but most of the time, it was volunteers with no education about the Bible or about history. They were members of local churches who felt the need to minister to inmates who needed salvation. While they meant well, and they brought love and acceptance to a marginalized group of men who had never felt love or acceptance, they also often taught very flawed lessons on the Bible, because that was how they had received the messages from their churches or Bible studies.

For example, they would preach that Jesus said, "Judge not, lest ye be judged." They would use this to tell everyone that they should not judge others. The first flaw in this lesson is that they never mentioned the *rest of the verse*, "For by the same measure which you judge others, so shall you be judged." The second flaw in this is that it is blatantly backward. Religion, and specifically the Bible, explicitly calls for people to judge one another, as a form of accountability. There is an entire book of the Bible *called* Judges! The correct lesson would be not to be a hypocrite. Do not condemn someone for stealing while you are rummaging through their belongings stealing from them, because your position will crumble when they shift the focus onto you doing the same thing, but absolutely call them out on stealing if you are not a thief, as a form of accountability

Also, as a Jew, it was agonizing for me to sit through a service about Passover or Yom Kippur, taught by laypeople, distorted through a Christian lens. Passover is not about the foretelling of Jesus being born. "The killing of the firstborn in Egypt was really a prophesy foretelling the killing of God's firstborn son on the cross!" and "Moses leading the Jewish people was foreshadowing for the baptism of John! Can I get an *amen!*" They always presented this in the stereotypical southern Baptist, shouting style of preaching *at* people rather than teaching *to* people. The only thing they got right was that the last supper was Jesus—*an orthodox Jewish rabbi*—observing the Passover.

I started bringing books to the services, which I put inside my Bible so I could sit in the back and read, pretending to be following along with the New Testament while I was actually reading about vampires and dragons, or about the Federation Starship *Enterprise* and the adventures of Spock and Captain Kirk.

On New Year's Eve, Johnny disappeared at the beginning of the service. There was no sign of him during the set. I thought he had a broken string break or something. Turned out, he'd had a tantrum and quit the band and was sitting in the music closet playing "Johnny B. Goode" through the entire service. I did not realize it, but apparently, he had been pretending to play but not actually playing anything, for weeks.

As we were wrapping up cords and putting away the equipment, Marcus came up to me and handed me three printouts.

"You need to learn these patterns by tomorrow," he said. "You are now our lead guitarist."

Panic hit me like a baseball bat to the face. Lead! I barely knew how to play rhythm. I had less than two year's experience, and most of that was self-taught.

"Excuse me?" I began. "I don't think this is a good idea." I know that I must have looked like a deer staring into headlights.

"And that is why I had Chaplain Watts print these out for you," Marcus responded matter-of-factly. "This is the major pentatonic diagonal pattern that everyone uses for lead. This other one is the minor pentatonic diagonal pattern. You cannot play a wrong note as long as you stay in the pattern."

"OK," I said. "But what about this last one? It looks completely different from the others?"

"That's the blues scale. That's all I know. Stick to the patterns and you'll be fine."

On New Year's Day, we set up for church service. I made sure that the printouts were on a music stand in front of me. I said a quick prayer that I would not embarrass myself too badly and made sure that my guitar was tuned.

When we started playing, I tried to stick to playing rhythm as best as I could. This wasn't too bad. We didn't really need a lead guitar anyway. It was blues, jazz, and southern gospel.

Then Dexter decided that I need an opportunity to do a solo because he was leaving and this was his last real gig. My life flashed before my eyes, my skin started to burn, and I knew I had to be fire engine red. I started sweating profusely as I tried to play the pattern, but the paper in front of me was swimming and swirling.

"Ting, tang, twang, wowow, chirp, twang!" My guitar made some noises that did not even remotely sound like music. I turned even more red and swore that the fires of hell were consuming me. Every eye was on me, I could feel it; everyone was laughing at me or gasping in disgusted horror at the horrible sounds coming from my guitar.

Suddenly, the moment passed, and I was no longer on the spot. I breathed a sigh of relief and resumed playing rhythm. After the set was over, the sound guy came up to the stage and told me not to worry—no one heard me crash and burn. Apparently, as soon as I started playing, he turned my sound off so no one but me could hear it!

This was the series of events that played out at every service for the next two weeks, until one day he didn't turn me down, and I had a standing ovation—I sounded pretty darn good!

Since I was playing with the praise band, no one in alpha dorm had any issue with me anymore. I must be a goodie-goodie because I was on the praise band, so I fit right in with the crowd of people in the faith-based dorm. Unfortunately for me, almost every person in the dorm was a child molester, here because this was the only place where they were safe from the other inmates. I made it for a few months before someone got too comfortable and started telling me that the father of his victim was in the next dorm over. I made the mistake of pretending to care, so he then told me that the father of his victim had HIV from sharing needles, and his daughter had been born with AIDS, which is how he caught AIDS. I was not really paying attention until he pointed out the father of his victim who could not have been a day over thirty years old. My brain kicked into overdrive and did some quick math. If the father was thirty and he got pregnant at fourteen years old, at best the victim was fifteen years old. At best.

"Dude," I began, "I do not want to hear about you catching AIDS from a teenage girl."

"Oh no," he responded. "She was not a teenager. She was eighteen months old. That's how they convicted me, saying the virus was identical and I could only have gotten it from the baby. Really, I was having an affair with his wife."

Everything seemed to slow down. All the noise in the dorm faded away and all I heard was a ringing sound. I saw his Adam's apple in his vulture-like neck jutting out, and I could see his heart beat in his carotid artery pulsing in the side of his neck. He was taller than me, but gangly and sickly, like maybe if Lurch from the Addams Family had a baby with a vulture.

All of a sudden all the noise came crashing back, time resumed, and I heard myself saying, "Get the fuck away from me, you disgusting sicko! Tighten up! Get in the grid!"

I yanked my shirt off and strode purposefully to the shower area, because in this dorm that was the only area not on camera and out of sight of the officer's station. I got to the shower area, and I was ready to kill this sicko. He fucking raped an eighteen-month-old baby, and they convicted him because the strain of HIV that he got was identical to the HIV the baby had been born with, which was different than the strain the parents had from using needles. My blood was boiling. I normally didn't care what anyone did that got them here; police are corrupt, and the court system was broken, without any concern for truth or for justice, and you could say you were anyone you wanted in here because there was really no way for me to verify or disprove that you were what you say you were. Child molesters almost always made up some story about being caught with weed or getting a DUI where no one got hurt, something that sounded victimless and innocent, but plausible for Florida.

Not this guy, though.

He just admitted to my face that he raped a year-and-a-half-old baby and caught AIDS from that baby. God had to be punishing this asshole, but I had the uncontrollable urge to be the hand of God and break every bone in his body this instant.

"Get the fuck over here!" I shouted again. "You cho-mo bitch. Fucking bragging about raping a baby! Get the fuck over here. Tighten up, pussy. Prey on someone your own size. When I knock you out, I am going to rape you with a broomstick in front of everyone. Get the fuck over here, bitch!" A "cho-mo" was the derogatory slang used to identify a child molester. Most of the population did not know what the word "molester" meant, but everyone knew what a cho-mo was.

I was steaming, raging inside that this guy hurt a child like that. After a few moments, when he had not come over, I decided that I would go to his side and fuck him up, cameras be damned.

"OK, you little bitch!" I said, "I am coming for you, and I hope they catch everything on camera. I am going to break every bone in your body and then make you choke on your own dick!"

As I started making my way across the dorm, a stocky, young, white man called nicknamed Country stepped in front of me.

"Don't do it, Bork. He isn't worth it. You can't change him, only change your release date." He grabbed me by the biceps as I tried to push past him.

"Get your fucking hands off of me," I snarled. "Or I will fuck you up too."

I saw at least three different emotions flicker across his face in an instant, and he settled on the one that required a display of machismo.

"I don't know who the fuck you think you are," he started, "but get in the grid. Ain't no one threatens me in this dorm." He yanked his shirt off and headed to the shower.

Now what was I supposed to do? Chase the cho-mo while ignoring the call out to the shower? Fight the scrawny harmless pedophile instead of the buff, white supremacist? That would bring me trouble because it would be perceived that I only fight the weak, afraid of anyone who can fight.

Before I could decide, three officers burst into the dorm, and the guard in the officer's station came over the loudspeaker ordering everyone to get on their bunks. I complied, as did Country. I was not sure whether they were here as a result of my commotion or for some other reason, but I tried to be as small as I could be to disappear.

The officers went directly to a specific bunk, to an inmate that everyone knew was smuggling tobacco into the dorms and selling it. Turns out, someone in here snitched on him, and they were here to search him and his locker. After going through his stuff, they found a couple hand-rolled cigarettes, and they had the inmate turn around, cuffed him up, and then they took him and his belongings out of the dorm. By now, I had cooled off enough that I was not going to kill the child molester, and Country and I were both cool enough to not fight, but there was definitely some hostility between us.

The next day, I returned from plumbing class and was told to roll it up. I was being moved to echo dorm, over in the T building. The place was full of two-man cells with solid doors and nothing on camera—the place where all the rapes and murders happened. A dungeon.

"Why am I being moved?" I asked the guard in the booth. "I'm part of the faith-based program here."

"Not anymore," the guard said. "According to this memo, Chaplain Ortega has removed you from the program."

I packed up my stuff, and headed over to echo dorm. I was terrified. This was where all the fights happened. This was where all the overdoses happened. This was the black hole of the compound. When I got to my new cell, I met my bunkmate. He looked a lot like Sin, glasses, slender, tattoos, dark hair.

"Bork." He looked up from his book.

How did he know me? I had only seen him once, the day I arrived.

"What's up, man?" I responded.

"Kicked you out of A dorm, huh?"

"Yeah, but I don't even know why yet," I replied.

"I do," he said. "You tried to fight a cho-mo. At least three people from the dorm ran to Chaplain Ortega first thing in the morning, including his office bitch, Asian Josh, all to snitch on you. They do not want anyone in the dorm who has an issue with pedophilia, because that is their safe place. You trying to fight one made them all scared."

"I'm sorry," I said. "You know my name. I can't seem to remember yours."

"Crause. Ernie Crause. Everyone calls me Crause. Nice to meet you, officially."

"I need to go speak to Chaplain Ortega. I need to tell him what happened and have him put me back in A dorm."

"Why do you want to be in A dorm?" Crause asked. "Place is full of child molesters and snitches. You have no freedom. Here, you can do whatever you want and come and go as you please. Also, Ortega won't listen to you. You can try, but I *will* say I told you so now, 'cause I am telling you so."

"Maybe true," I said. "But I was comfortable there. I had a routine. All the rest of the band is there."

"Nope," Crause said flatly.

"Nope?"

"Half of the band is in G dorm now," Crause replied. "They're lifers, and that is the lifer dorm. Trueblood. Gene. The Nazi guitarist. They all live in G dorm. Not alpha. Anyone who does real time knows that the two-man cells are the only way to do time. Open bay dorms are hard time even at the nicest compounds. That's where all the pride workers are housed too."

"Pride?" I asked.

"Yes, as in P-R-I-D-E, only paid jobs in Florida prison. PRIDE jobs pay like thirty cents an hour, highly coveted, generally given to those with life sentences or huge amounts of time that might as well be life. It's essentially voluntary slave labor."

"Yeah, OK," I said, "but I'm going to speak to the chaplain now anyway."

"Waste of time," Crause mumbled as he went back to reading his book.

Sure enough, before I got to Chaplain Ortega, Asian Josh stopped me and gave me a bunch of condescending bullshit about how the chaplain was a busy man and, if I wanted to speak to him, I needed put in a request form. I saw Marcus doing some paperwork in one of the chapel offices nearby, so I bypassed Asian Josh and went to Marcus.

"Hey, man," I started, "can you please get the chaplain to speak to me? He kicked me out of the faith-based dorm without even talking to me."

"I can try," Marcus told me. "But no promises. He's in a really bad mood today."

I waited while Marcus poked his head into the chaplain's office, and I could hear the chaplain speaking.

"Bork? Tell him I am *not* available. Oh and, Sumes, I do not think he's a good fit for the band. Tell him he's suspended for thirty days."

Marcus came back out.

"Sorry, man," he began. "The chaplain doesn't want to speak to right now, and he suspended you from the band."

"Yeah. I heard," I said. "Isn't there anything you can do?"

"Not today, but I'll try." Marcus said. "Keep coming to every service, support the band, show the chaplain you're still committed. Come to practices, but just do not touch an instrument. You're still part of the band, only suspended temporarily."

For the millionth time, I couldn't believe what was happening—I was being punished based on the hearsay of a child molester, not even given a chance to tell my side of the story. Even the broken and corrupt criminal court system gives you a *facade* of fairness.

When I got back to my new dorm, I submitted a request form to speak to the chaplain. One way or another, I would get my side heard.

For the next four weeks, I had an ungodly amount of free time. At the faith-based dorm, I could either go to plumbing class or some faith-based program learning platitudes and reading Christian pamphlets about how the only way I would ever be a good person was if I accepted Jesus into my life. Now, though, I had almost all-day every-day free to be on the rec yard or do whatever I wanted, because I now had nothing to do. For a few weeks, I spent time walking around on the rec yard, doing Tai Chi, and playing Dungeons & Dragons. Apparently, a group of the guys in E dorm had made dice from materials stolen from PRIDE, and they had all the prohibited books. These guys were not generally available during the day, as they were at work in PRIDE, but when they came back, my afternoons and evenings were filled with dragons and elves. I still went to the chapel services, but I picked and chose the ones I would endure. I didn't go to every single one, but I picked the ones that were the most fun or had someone who knew the Bible well enough for me to learn something. In the mornings, though, I ran the track. It hurt my back with every step, but it kept my stamina up, and if I was seen working out regularly, I was less likely to be a target.

On the rec yard, there was a guy who was always doing handstands and walking around on his hands. This guy spent every moment on the rec yard doing handstands. He would stand there for five minutes on his hands, not even a wobble in his balance. I tried to join him doing handstands a few times and realized very quickly that he had been practicing for years to get this good. I could not even make it thirty seconds. I stuck with doing Tai Chi with another guy who had years of kung fu and Tai Chi experience. It was peaceful, focusing on the Tai Chi and listening to the wind on the rec yard.

Before too long, though, I got bored.

I had no mental stimulation. I put a request in to Classification to be reassigned to the law library. I could type sixty words per minute, and was an avid reader, so maybe I could find something stimulating there.

About the time that I was scheduled for Classification to reassign me, I also got scheduled to meet with Chaplain Ortega. I got up to his office, and he made me wait outside in the heat for over an hour. Finally, when he let me in, he was very curt.

"Inmate Bork. How can I help you?"

"Well, Chaplain," I responded, "you can tell me why I was suspended from the band and kicked out of the faith-based program."

"Because you are violent and threatened to kill everyone," Chaplain told me. "Is that not the case?"

"I never threatened to kill anyone, nor have I engaged in any violence. One of the inmates started bragging to me about how he raped an *eighteen-month-old baby*, and I *wanted* to fight him. I *wanted* to hurt him. I never got a chance, though. Before you tell me that I was wrong for feeling that way, what is it that Jesus said about children? Matthew 18:10 says, 'See that you do not despise one of these little ones. For I tell you that their angels in heaven always see the face of my Father in heaven.' And Matthew 18:2–6 says, 'If anyone causes one of these little ones—those who believe in me—to stumble, it would be better for them to have a large millstone hung around their neck and to be drowned in the depths of the sea.' You would punish me for following the teaching of Jesus that you preach, and defend someone who lives the opposite of everything you preach?"

"OK," Chaplain said sheepishly, clearly cornered, "but what about Country? You going to fight him too?"

"No, sir," I responded. "I was going to defend the children, and he did the right thing by me, to prevent me from extending my sentence. Had he allowed me to hurt the child molester, I would probably have gotten additional charges. But in the moment, I couldn't see that and just saw someone who was defending a baby rapist."

"OK," Chaplain said. "You can return to playing with the praise band. Trueblood has been in here every day asking for you to be allowed to return. Would you like to return to the faith-based program? You had almost finished it."

"No, thanks," I answered. "I'm more comfortable in the two-man cells. More privacy, quieter. I get along well with my cellmate."

"OK," Chaplain said to me. He turned away and picked up the phone, indicating that the conversation was over.

I left and headed to my Classification appointment. This appointment was much less interesting. I was reassigned to the law library as the typist. At least, I would be able to work in the air-conditioning through the summer and stay in the heat during the winter.

My new position in the law library was a sweet gig, allowing me the ability to earn lots of currency, typing things for people. The civilian who ran the library was not abusive to the inmates. She treated everyone as normal people, no different than if we worked for her in any civilian job. She was polite and respectful, and recognized our humanity. Working for her was a sweet gig, an escape from prison for a few hours. As long as I typed all the legal documents that people submitted through the proper channels, she didn't care that I also typed other things for people. With that in mind, I charged two bags of coffee minimum to have someone skip the line and get their documents typed, plus a bag of coffee per page. I did not always have customers, but when I did, it was lucrative. I could bang out most documents in minutes when I could read their handwriting. Sometimes it was a little harder, but I have a sharp legal mind and could usually decipher what they were trying to say. I made grammatical corrections for them and ensured that their legal arguments were sound and cited valid laws and cases. I was not supposed to, because I was not a law clerk, just a typist. But those who gave me their documents and let me fix them tended to have better outcomes than those who did not, and word spread.

Working in the library had another perk—unlimited access to books. I could check out any books that I wanted, as many as I wanted. I devoured then, two a day, taking a book with me to the chow hall and to the chapel, running on the rec yard with a book, reading through every count time. I consumed nearly a dozen books a week. *Hunger Games, Harry Potter, Dante's Inferno, The Dresden Files,* Wheel of Time series, *Catcher in the Rye, David Copperfield, Tale of Two Cities, Jack Reacher.* I read everything. I went through all the fantasy, all of the science fiction, all of the action, into all of the classics, through all of Stephen King's horrors, then into romance like *True Blood, Outlander,* and works by Jane Austen, Nicholas Sparks, Lynsey Sands, and Sandra Hill. Plus, I could charge two dollars per book to get and return books for inmates who couldn't get to the library. Sweet, easy money.

Everything was great for a few months. My job assignment was low stress, peaceful, and climate controlled. My bunkmate was a really chill person who kept all his drug use and illicit activities outside the cell because you don't shit where you sleep, and I was back on the praise band.

One week, there was a change in facility staff because of some rumor about the librarian having sexual relations with an inmate, and the librarian was replaced by a mean, old hag from another compound, who hated Jews, hated men, and made it her mission to "clean up" the library. She started throwing away hundreds of books, trying to eliminate 80 percent of the books on the compound, and she started firing the inmates who worked in the library. She felt that there only needed to be one law clerk and one library clerk, and the law clerk could handle any typing that was needed. I found myself out of a job along with all of the other library staff. The next day, the compound had a shakedown, and the officers targeted the remaining and former library staff specifically, confiscating any books that any of us had, even catching one of the inmates with a can of tobacco and a cell phone.

* * *

This was the first time that I had started to feel real hope, an all-around sense of there being light at the end of the tunnel, not just in part of my day but in my entire situation. Although I was still in prison, my overall situation had generally become tolerable. In other locations, I had something that made the time tolerable like the carpentry program, but I was still in hell the rest of the time. Or the ultimate Frisbee and chapel band, but I was still in hell the rest of the time. Finally, I had an all-around sensation that I *was* going to survive, that there was nothing too terrible that was going to happen to me anymore despite still being incarcerated.

Then the hope was crushed *again*.

You can only dangle a piece of meat in front of an abused, starving lion so many times before he goes ballistic, before something in his soul breaks. When that moment finally comes, the despair is so much darker even than during the abuse. There is nothing darker than the loss of hope, except maybe the fallout after it's yanked away.

From arriving at Polk till now, I had truly thought things were getting better. I allowed myself to believe that it was better, that the worst was behind me. When the realization dawned on me that I was wrong and the darkness was not yet at its darkest, something inside me broke. I hit rock bottom.

Not everyone knows what rock bottom feels like, although we have all heard the term used.

This is what it feels like: an overwhelming hopelessness, so heavy, that it crushes you, and takes the air out of your lungs. The despair of knowing that your situation is insurmountable, that there's no way out, and that you are powerless. Feeling completely out of control, with no input or ability to affect your own life, relationships, or your environment. It comes with heavy waves of sadness, anger, anxiety, laced with shame. Hitting, rock bottom affects you physically. You lose your desire to eat, because food loses its flavor. Everything tastes like cardboard or dirt. You're unable to sleep because the weight of your despair is crushing you. Why sleep? Even in dreams you have no control over anything, and the suffering was worse there. For me, hitting rock bottom put me lower than being suicidal. Yes, I wanted to die to escape, but the level of hopelessness was so extreme that I had even lost hope that suicide would eliminate my suffering.

Being powerless made me angry. Feeling trapped made me angry. Knowing that I was being punished for what I had done but that others who were doing worst things than me were not being held accountable, that injustice made me angry. My moment of hitting rock bottom was also my moment where, having nothing left to lose, I had everything to gain by fighting, by standing up for what's right. I don't mean fighting with my fists; hitting rock bottom meant that I had nothing to lose by challenging the establishment and the people in power. There was nothing worse they could do to me other than kill me, and I already saw dying as a better option than continuing as I was. There was no outcome that could've been worse than rock bottom.

Everything was going to change. I was going to make sure that the people who hurt me would never be able to hurt anyone else in the same way. Hitting rock bottom became the catalyst for an inevitable nuclear reaction that I was going to initiate.

I started writing to the defense lawyer who had represented me and took pictures of my bruises and my injuries when he came to visit me. I started gathering all my records, and I kept impeccable records. I kept a journal documenting the day and the time of each beating, of each time I was denied food, of each time I was forced to drink from a toilet or denied medical attention. I documented who was responsible or involved in the action, what steps I took to address it. Every time I sent a grievance or a request form, it was documented. I had pages and pages of neatly detailed notes documenting everything.

I obtained the form from the law library for a Federal Section 1983 Civil Rights lawsuit. This lawsuit was designed to bring about sweeping change and stop civil rights violations, or cruel and unusual punishment. This type of lawsuit was never designed to result in personal financial gain or payouts. And I wanted every officer at that jail who was involved in hurting me to be held accountable. I wanted them to lose that freedom and be charged with assault and battery, human rights violations even. I didn't care about getting paid. I wasn't even in that facility anymore. But other human beings were still there, and there was no living creature on earth that should ever be abused in that manner. There was no crime so horrible that deserved that type of torture.

I spent hours in the law library and reading case law, looking for precedent and other similar cases throughout the United States and over the last hundred years. I wanted to hit them with everything the legal system would allow me to.

Eventually, I filed a lawsuit. I named names. I shared the gory details. I presented clear and definitive proof as well as clear definitive arguments as to why what was going on was cruel and unusual punishment and violated multiple constitutional protections that every American is entitled to even if they've committed murder or treason. I did not start with a demand for money. I demanded change. I wanted every officer involved to be fired and prevented from ever working in law enforcement again. I wanted the medical staff involved to lose their medical certifications and never be able to work in healthcare again. I wanted a public apology. And most of all, I wanted my freedom. I wanted the courts to decide that what I had endured was greater than the five-year prison sentence that I had been given and have them terminate my sentence as completed so that I could go home.

When it became clear that I was not going to be receiving my freedom in exchange for winning or dropping my lawsuit, I modified my request to include financial compensation. This type of lawsuit was not intended for financial compensation or penalties, but I pushed for it anyway. I requested summary judgment, hoping that the judge would award in my favor by default if the jail didn't bother to respond. I wanted the jail shut down. I wanted the world to know what had happened. I wanted Oprah to hear about it and to come interview me.

It took time, but eventually my complaint was heard by the courts, and it rang loud enough for the prison and the jails to take notice even up to the highest levels of their corporate staff. They had teams of six hundred dollar an hour attorneys—not one attorney, not two attorneys, entire teams of six hundred dollar an hour attorneys come to take my deposition to see if I was a legitimate threat.

After my deposition, the lead attorney spoke to me, off the record. He shook my hand and told me that I was not what he was expecting and that he was terribly sorry for what had happened to me. He told me that he was expecting to come in and go through the motions of a deposition, for a case that would not go anywhere because the plaintiff was just an uneducated, ignorant inmate. He told me that it's a shame that I had been convicted of a felony because I would have made a phenomenal attorney and he would've loved to have had me on his team.

There were additional visits from the opposing attorneys as my lawsuit gained steam and was taken seriously. I spent as many hours in the law library as I could, and although my access to applicable legal materials was limited because the law library is set up specifically for state criminal law and not for federal or civil law, I was relentless, determined, and had nothing to lose.

What happened to me as I was hyperfocused on getting justice was that I found purpose. The determination to get justice and to protect others from suffering the same way that I had at the hands of those with the power to hurt became my fire. The hopelessness was replaced with a burning rage, a white-hot fire of righteousness. I became a crusader, and this was my crusade. It overpowered the despair, the hopelessness, and it became the light at the end of the tunnel for me. I was going to see daylight again. I was going to hold bad people accountable for what they did. I was going to protect others even if they didn't know me. I was going to succeed, or I was going to die trying.

My grandmother would be proud of me, refusing to give up in this as she refused to give up when she was in the concentration camps and stared death in the face every day. My grandfather would be proud, because instead of giving up, he was teaching Jews to urinate into the guidance systems of the V2 rockets before sealing them, saving hundreds of thousands of British lives even while the Nazis held a gun to his head. He would give up his food to those around him to make sure everyone had something. He protected others who couldn't protect themselves, or didn't even know they needed protecting, with total disregard for himself. Yes, my grandparents would be proud of my determination to see this through!

While I am prohibited from discussing the details of the outcome because both parties signed a confidentiality agreement, I can say that the court did not revoke my conviction or sentence. The lawsuit that I filed was not the correct category to have any legal bearing on my freedom.

But I can say that I have periodically communicated with individuals who are or were incarcerated there, and to the best of my knowledge, there have not been any further incidents of abuse at that jail since. Also, Oprah never came to see me.

CRASH DUMMIES
AND LOAN SHARKS

The inmate in the cell next to me, Miguel, and the inmate in the cell across the hall from me, Carlos, both worked in laundry, and they'd been asking me to come work laundry with them for a few weeks. There was an opening there because someone recently went home, and they knew I kept my head down and didn't draw attention. I was the perfect person to work with because I was the one guy always dismissed by officers looking for wrongdoing. That was good business, and the fact is that I was honest and forthright in all my business dealings. Carlos was the shot caller for the Nÿetas, a Latin gang on the compound, and Miguel was the gang's "treasurer," or so he said. Miguel was also the main guy in laundry, and Carlos was the number two, running the supply side. They put in a good word for me with Sergeant Moore and Officer Smith. Moore was a gunnery sergeant in the Marine Corps Reserves, and he'd noticed my Marine Corps tattoos.

I went to Classification along with all the other former library staff and got assigned to laundry. I was not really fond of the idea that I would be washing skid marks out of grown men's underwear, but I knew that there was profit to be made and perks to be had working there.

After a few weeks in laundry, Miguel decided he wanted to make an entrepreneur out of me. I managed to set up a client list of inmates in the dorm who paid me for "special wash" (i.e., they got a wash every ten sets of clothing instead of three hundred).

"Bork" Miguel said, "come into my room for a minute. I want to ask you something."

"Sure," I said. "But I'm not gay. You have to talk to Crause about that."

"Yeah, yeah," Miguel said. "Everyone knows that white boys are all gay. What I want to know is whether or not you're a storeman. You can hustle better than anyone I seen in ten years locked up. Why don't you run a store?"

"Because I don't want to have to fight people when they fail to pay me," I said. "And you and I both know that, for no reason other than being white, I *will* be forced to. All the black gang members will see this as a beautiful opportunity to take from the white man without consequence, because the white man owes them."

"So what? I know you can fight. I called a brother of mine at Century. He saw you take out eight Cutthroat members at once. You ain't afraid to fight, and you can fucking fight. You only have to one time—then everyone'll pay you. Make me a list of everything you need to start your store, *ese*. I'll go to the canteen tomorrow and get you a hundred dollars."

"If you say so," I said. "And what happens when someone doesn't pay me what I owe you?"

"Then you will fight them," Miguel answered as he began to walk away. "One time. You already knew that. Keep this between me and you. I don't want any of my brothers to know that I funded you, 'cause then they'll expect a hookup, and you can't make any money like that."

"And just what'll I owe you for this loan?" I asked.

"Give me back double," Miguel said over his shoulder. "Within two weeks."

Later that evening, I made a list of the high-demand items that I thought I needed in order to make money as a storeman. A storeman was essentially a loan shark. I had a locker full of goods, so when an inmate's family gave them fifty dollars at the beginning of the month, usually when they got their welfare checks, they'd blow it in under three weeks. After that, they could come borrow from me. There was a catch, because nothing in prison was free: whatever they borrowed from me, they had to pay back double within seven days. On the seventh day, it doubled again. On the fourteenth day, it doubled yet again. On the twenty-first day, another doubling. On the twenty-eighth day, I broke a bone to grant them another week, but it still doubled again. For example, someone borrowed one ramen soup for two back on the first week. Second week, two became four, then four became eight, then eight became sixteen. By week five, they owed me thirty-two soups and a broken bone.

Very simple. Loan shark.

I kept a composition notebook where I wrote poetry, and on a random page in the middle, I started a handwritten spreadsheet. My spreadsheet had columns for the following information:

- name and cell number of borrower

- date borrowed.

- dollar amount borrowed

- detailed breakdown of what was borrowed

- amount paid back (as any outstanding balance continued to double exponentially)

I have serious OCD, and so I kept track of every penny I was owed or owed others.

Something I discovered early on was that I could make 20 percent profit on reselling coffee if I broke it down into single-serve portions. Drug dealers had a method that worked for sales, and I started applying that. A bag of coffee cost six dollars. I could smuggle food service gloves out of the chow hall or from laundry and fill each finger with 2 spoonfuls. Tear the finger off the glove, fill with coffee using a sheet of paper as a funnel, and tie a knot into each finger. Boom! I had a product I could sell for seventy cents each.

I could do what everyone else did and get twenty fingers (reselling a six-dollar bag of coffee for fourteen dollars), or I could make them a little bigger and get twelve fingers (reselling a six-dollar bag of coffee for $8.40). Too much competition in a saturated market to sell at the same quantity and price as everyone else, but if I offered nearly 50 percent more than my competitors for the same price, I would be the clear choice. It was Economics 101, in a rubber glove.

On the list that I gave Miguel, I included five bags of coffee with this approach in mind. I made the list full of lower price items, such as cookies and soups, because I knew that psychologically, customers would be more likely to borrow things that are not expensive to pay back—those items provided the greatest marginal utility. Also, if they didn't pay up even after I fought them, it would be easier to replenish inexpensive items out of my easy profits.

Next afternoon, Miguel held true to his word. When the rec yard closed and everyone came inside for count, Miguel walked into my room and dropped a large laundry bag full of canteen onto my bunk.

"Here ya go, Bork," he said. "You didn't get it from me. Don't let me down. Two weeks, same list, doubled."

"Thanks," I said, hoping my sarcasm wasn't too obvious. "I got you."

As Miguel walked out of my room, Crause walked back in from the rec yard.

"Dayum, boy!" he exclaimed. "You rich. Bank! Lemme hold something."

"No problem, but I need two back," I responded.

"Two back?" Crause asked. "What, you think you are a store-man now or something?"

"Actually," I said, "yeah. That is exactly what I am. I have an investor, though, so I can *not* play with the product."

"A'ight," Crause said. "I'll support your store. I'm your first customer. Lemme hold a rack of cookies. Strawberry. I got you tomorrow."

"Cool," I said as I handed him a rack of strawberry creme duplex cookies. Immediately, I pulled out my composition notebook and wrote:

Crause, E2107, 08/07/2016, $1.00, 1 cookie (strawberry)

"What are you doing!" Crause said.

"Keeping track of every transaction," I said. "This way, no one can lie about what they owe and when they owe it. Also, this way I can keep track of my business. I have a separate page for all my special wash customers too."

"Shit," Crause replied, "you are serious about this then."

"Oh yeah," I said. "And when I break someone's leg over a two-cent sugar packet, they will realize just how serious."

"*Damn.*" Crause ate another cookie.

During count, I portioned out two bags of coffee into fingers.

"You're making them too big," Crause said.

"Nope. I'm making sure that I have a better deal than anyone else. I might make less profit per bag of coffee, but I won't waste as much time trying to sell it, and I'll get the attention of everyone who needs a storeman. Double whammy on the marketing and advertising. Plus, even if I make a little less per transaction, I'll have significantly more transactions and that means volume—and more money."

"If you say so. Let me get a coffee bomb."

"OK," I responded. "But do not make me hurt you to get paid. I like you as a roommate. Would be a shame to have to break in and train a new roomie."

"Clear count! Clear count!" the officer shouted over the loudspeakers.

"Well," I said, "here goes. Wish me luck."

"Get it, boi," Crause said.

I walked out of my cell with a coffee bag full of coffee bombs and started shouting like a street vendor hawking his wares,

"Coffee bombs! Coffee bombs! Get your big, fat coffee bombs! Biggest coffee bombs on the compound! Coffee bombs for sale!"

As I walked through the halls of the dorm, through the common area and TV area on the first floor and second floors, a bunch of the older men stopped me.

"Lemme see your bombs" was the common response. I sold out quickly. Apparently, these were the biggest coffee bombs anyone had ever seen. They thought they were taking advantage of the young white boy who didn't know better. They didn't realize that their skimpy let's-get-each-customer-for-the-most-money-with-the-least-value approach was small-minded. I was thinking big picture, not instant gratification. And I already knew exactly what my profit margins were. I needed ten ramen soups to trade for a full bag of coffee, and I was getting a minimum of twelve coffee bombs per bag. The faster I could sell out, the faster I could move to another bag and do it again.

I continued to walk the dorm, poking my head into the rooms of the guys who I knew didn't have much money or hustles. They were the best market because they could hustle up a soup or two, but could never afford to get a six-dollar bag of coffee (which was like coming up with six hundred bucks in the real world). Easy customers.

"Hey, Bork!" A random inmate whose name I didn't know shouted. "Lemme get a coffee bomb, and I'll pay you tomorrow."

"No, sir," I responded. "I am running a store, so if you do not have cash in hand right now, it will be double to pay me later."

"Fuck that!" He stormed off. This happened about ten times in twenty minutes with different guys, which was about how long it took me to sell all twelve of the coffee bombs.

I headed back to my room to drop all of the soups in my locker and found Crause reading a book.

"Sold out already?"

"Yup."

"Damn that was fast," Crause said. "What are you going to do now?"

"I am going to take nine soups and get a bag of coffee to do it again."

"You know you need ten soups to trade for a bag of coffee, right?"

"Well," I said, "not if I shop around. I bet I can find someone who'll do it for nine."

I took nine soups around the dorm, looking for some the older guys who work for PRIDE. I knew they had consistent income and usually full lockers. If I could get a bag of coffee as an even trade for nine soups anywhere, it would be from these guys, because it might save them a trip to the canteen, standing in line in the heat for an hour.

Eventually, I found Tony alone in his room—he was an older black man who liked younger white boys and had been locked up for twenty-six years. He'd been flirting with me and pursuing me for nearly a year, especially after I started working in the library with him.

"Hey, Tony," I started. "How are you?"

"Hey, Bork." Tony always spoke softly, very feminine, despite looking like Dwayne "The Rock" Johnson. "How's it going?"

"Pretty good, Tony. I was just wondering if you could do me a favor?"

"Sure!" Tony said. "What do you need? You hungry? I can make you a bowl of food if you want to eat with me?" This was how Tony won them over. He offered to share his food with hungry young men and asked nothing in return. For a while. You ate with him enough times, though, and you owed him. That's how it goes in prison. If you weren't careful and you owed someone something that you couldn't pay back, you ended up getting raped.

"No, thanks, Tony." I said. "I'm here on business actually."

"Really? What can I do for you? You know I will support you in anything you do."

"Of course, you would, Tony. I have nine soups. I want to trade them for a bag of coffee. Interested?"

"Normally, I get ten soups for a bag," he said matter-of-factly. "But for you, I will make an exception." He reached into his locker and pulled out a bag of coffee, then tossed it to me.

"Thanks, Tony," I said as I dumped the pile of soups on his bunk.

As I turned to leave, Tony said, "You wanna stay and eat? I made too much."

I was tempted, because I *was* hungry. And I knew I could beat Tony in a fight if he ever tried to rape me. Still, did I want the reputation of being his boy toy?

Finally, I said, "Sure, why not."

Do not judge me. Until you know what it feels like to be chronically hungry and malnourished, you can't understand.

"Cool," Tony said. "Go get your bowl and come on back."

I went back to my cell with the coffee to get my bowl. Crause was shocked that I managed to trade nine soups for a bag of coffee because in his mind, who would take a twenty-nine-cent loss on a trade like that?

"Where are you going with that bowl?" he asked.

"I am going to eat with Tony," I replied.

"Ah," Crause said. "Now I understand. Smart, but dangerous. Be careful, white boy. Tony has a twelve-inch monster cock."

"Dude," I responded, "how do you even know that? And, no, I am not ever going to have sex with Tony, or any other man. Gonna have to kill me first."

"Sure," Crause said. "That's what they all say. I'll get an extra pillow for you to sit on."

"Fuck you, dude," I said, laughing as I walked out.

It didn't take long before word spread that there was a new storeman in the dorm, and I had a few dozen names on my list of people who had borrowed from me. Most pay back double within a few days because they had to wait a few weeks when their monthly money from their families. My five best customers were Crause; a little black kid not a day over twenty that everyone called Swift; an older white supremacist with a giant red-and-black swastika on the back of his head named JC who was a lifelong member of the gang known as Unforgiven; his smoking-buddy Christopher; a young nineteen-year-old black drug addict; and a white guy called Twitch in his early twenties who spent his days looking for spice, the synthetic marijuana that makes you see Satan. Eventually, I stopped loaning to Crause and just gave him whatever he wanted because I knew he would pay me back within twenty-four hours, and he was my roommate.

Also, he made sure I didn't get robbed when I wasn't in the dorm.

Just thirteen days after Miguel gave me the start-up funds for the store, I walked into his room with a laundry bag nearly bursting at the seams.

"Here you go, big dog," I said, handing him the bag. "Everything you gave me, times two, plus a little extra for giving me the push to do it."

"Bork!" Miguel says. "My man! I never doubted you for a second. You are the craziest hustler I have seen in ten years. You're good business. I will put out the word to everyone that you're good business."

"Thanks, buddy."

As I was walking out of his room, large black Sergeant Gaines came into the dorm.

"One time! One time!" inmates started shouting, like the officers didn't know the code for "There's an officer coming. Put away all your illicit stuff and pretend to be innocent."

I normally ignored when this happened because I did not partake of illicit behaviors such as smoking, using drugs or having gay sex using mayonnaise as lube, but Sergeant Gaines came straight for my room.

"Inmate Bork, you are Crause's roommate, right? Pack up Crause's stuff and bring it to me at the officer's station." He turned around and walked off.

Shit. What did Crause get himself into? He was so good about keeping his smoking and cell phone activity away from the room. I thought maybe he got caught in another dorm with one of his boyfriends. While I was packing up his stuff, five different people all came to the room claiming that Crause owed them money or that stuff in his locker belonged to them.

"Yeah?" I said. "You'll have to take that up with him when he gets out of confinement, because I don't know anything about his business."

I took all of Crause's belongings to Sergeant Gaines in the officer station and asked him for details. Turns out I was on the money—he had been caught in the wrong place without authorization. At least, he'd be out of confinement in a few days since it wasn't a serious offense, just failure to be obedient.

The next day, roaming the compound collecting laundry from medical and other areas, I saw Sergeant Gaines having a private conversation with one of the inmates who worked in the chow hall. I watched as Gaines discreetly handed the inmate two cell phones, a can of chewing tobacco, a pack of cigarettes, and a bag of what I assumed to be marijuana but was probably spice.

I knew Gaines was dirty, and I'd heard rumors that he brought phones in. I had even heard that he would confiscate the phone if he wasn't paid fast enough, then resell it to another inmate. I had never personally witnessed it until now, though. As he looked up and saw me, I put my head down and kept walking, acting like I didn't see him at all. I did not want him coming around to harass me just because I was unlucky enough to witness him breaking the law. Then again, now I knew where Crause got all the tobacco he was always selling and hustling.

I got to enjoy having a cell to myself for all of two days, then a little white drug addict was assigned to my room. This was no good—when he got into trouble they would probably take me to confinement simply by association, and then I'd lose months of accumulated gain time that should have shortened my sentence. I simply could not allow some little kid to extend my sentence by months.

The new roommate's name was Chris. He was tiny and young, twenty-one years young, maybe five feet three, blond, and totally brain-dead. He was already high as he walked into the room—now how the hell did he get high on the short walk from being released from confinement to here? He dropped his bag of belongings on the floor, introduced himself, and said, "You smoke? You know where I can get some K-2."

"No," I responded. "I do not smoke, I do not know where you can get drugs, and I promise you that if you bring any drugs, phones, or tobacco into this room or get high in here, that I will knock you out and rape you."

"Jesus!" Chris replied. "That is really fucked up, dude. You won't really do that."

"Try me and find out." I stared him down.

This one was going to be trouble, or so I thought.

But actually, aside from being high all the time, Chris was not a bad roommate. He didn't have anything, because as soon as he got his hands on anything of value, it immediately got traded for drugs. He got assigned to working in the kitchen for the early-morning shift, which was really nice for him because it gave him an opportunity to steal lots of contraband from the chow hall and sell it for drugs. His first day in the kitchen, he brought back a bread bag full of oatmeal.

"How much do you want for the oatmeal?" I asked him.

"A bag of coffee," Chris answered.

"I'll give you three racks of cookies," I countered. "Three dollars."

"Deal," Chris answered.

Now I could put peanut butter in my oatmeal, drop in a handful of trail mix, and I would have a heavy, healthy, protein-packed, delicious meal. I think that I had enough to last me a week, three bowls per day.

This was a pattern that repeated itself every day for two weeks: Chris smuggled food out of the chow hall—peppers, onions, tomatoes, bananas, oatmeal—and I had first dibs on buying it. Since I had a steady supply of income from working in laundry and being the storeman, I generally bought everything he brought back after haggling him way down on price, then I resold half of it for double and kept the other half for myself.

One morning, Chris refused to get up for work when the officers came to wake him at 3:00 a.m. The officer tried three times to get him up, but then moved on. After we came back from breakfast a few hours later, two officers came to the room and told him to cuff up. Off he went to confinement as I packed up yet another roommate's belongings.

One week later, I was assigned yet another roommate. I went through the same set of introductions. His name was Swish, and he was the new inmate barber. He looked white and was covered in tattoos. While he seemed all right, I had to tell him the same thing I told Chris: "I don't smoke, I don't know where you can get drugs, and I promise you that if you bring any drugs, phones, or tobacco into this room or get high in here, I will knock you out and fuck you in the ass."

"I am a Golden Gloves boxer," Swish retorted. "You think you can take me?"

"Try me and find out." I stared him down, and he walked away. This one was gonna be trouble too. Lack of respect was written all over his face.

The first week that Swish was my roommate, things were OK, but it wasn't long before he got comfortable and started bringing tobacco into the room, rolling cigarettes, and smoking by the window to keep the smell out.

"Bro," I started as I sat up and got off my bunk, "I warned you about bringing contraband into my room. *If you play with my release date, I am going to have to hurt you.* Fair warning."

Swish turned to me from the end of his bunk where he was rolling another cigarette, and as he was licking the paper to finish the roll, he smirked and asked, "What are you going to do about it?"

"Flush it now," I said, "Or I will."

Swish laughed as he finished rolling the cigarette and pulled out a battery and a paper clip to light it with. I rolled my eyes and acted like I was turning away from him, then snapped around and smashed my fist into his eye. Swish stumbled back, dropping the cigarette conveniently right into the toilet, and then came back swinging. He definitely had some experience boxing, but I don't know if he really was Golden Gloves. He threw a frenzy of blows—left jab, right jab, left jab, right uppercut, left jab, right hook. I blocked and deflected every punch using Mr. Miyagi–style wax-on/wax-off circles, then shot both of my hands in like I was diving into a swimming pool. I grabbed him by the back of the head, both of my elbows tight against his chest in a clinch. As I yanked his head down, I drove my right knee up into his chest one time. The second time I went to drive my knee up as I pulled his head down, he blocked down with both of his arms.

I guess he really didn't like the feeling of my knee slamming into his chest.

I used this opportunity to let go of his head with my right hand, and as he pulled his head back up, I drove my elbow into his jaw.

Swish stumbled backward, reeling from the impact of my elbow. I was already moving forward as he straightened up, and we both punched with our right hands at exactly the same time. His fist landed solidly on my left eye, and my fist landed solidly on his collarbone. Swish apparently realized he was outclassed and turned to run out of the room. I grabbed his right wrist, and as he got to the door, I bent his arm at the elbow and brought his wrist and hand tight to my chest in a reverse wristlock come-along. Most people would see this and have called it a chicken wing, but regardless of what anyone called it, it was sufficient to control the two-hundred-pound dude enough for me to stop him from leaving the room.

While Swish was trying to get out, I applied pressure to his wrist with my right hand as I reached my left arm around his throat. I went to choke him, then realized that I could yank the door shut first. I used my left hand to grab the door in front of his face and pulled hard to the left, nearly shutting the steel door on his fingers as he was trying to pull himself out of the room.

As my chest was already against his back, and my left arm was already around the front of his throat, I let go of his wrist and applied all the pressure I could muster into choking the life out of him—a military variation of the MMA rear-naked choke, known as the figure-four variation. My left arm was around his neck and grabbing high up on my right shoulder. My right hand was on the back of his head, and I put my left ear on the back of my right hand, tucking my chin and face into the pocket of my right shoulder to keep it protected.

I stepped backward while applying pressure with my head and arms, "listening" to him sleep. It took about three seconds, but Swish stopped his frantic struggling, and his entire body went limp. I held the choke for an extra "one Mississippi" before laying him face down on the floor. I pushed his legs apart and kicked him in the asshole as hard as I could five times before pulling his pants down to his knees. I grabbed a packet of mayonnaise as he started stirring, ripped it open, and squirted it on his bare ass, tossing the wrapper into the toilet.

"Uhhhng," Swish groaned as he pushed himself up.

I turned to the cell door and saw my neighbor from across the hall standing there with a big smile. His name was also Joshua, so I shouted through the door to him.

"Hey, Josh! Please have the CO buzz my door. I shut it by mistake."

"Hahahahaha!" Joshua laughed loudly. "That's exactly what happened. I'm going now. Got you."

"Did you fucking rape me, dude!" Swish asked in a panic as he wiped mayo off his ass and pulled his pants up.

"I warned you," I replied. "Keep the drugs, phones, and tobacco out of my fucking room, or we will repeat today's performance."

Clank-clank-clank! Our door buzzed open as Josh walked up to the door.

"Everyone good in here?" Josh asked.

"Yes," I replied.

Swish asked, "Dude, did he really rape me?"

Josh looked from me to Swish, then back at me.

"I don't know. Does your ass hurt?"

"Fuck you, dude!" Swish said. "I am a man. If he raped me, you owe it to me to tell me!"

"I do not owe you shit, cracker," Josh said. "If you got your ass beat and raped, that's on you. I ain't saying shit." Josh turned to me. "Thanks for the show, Bork. Very entertaining." He chuckled as he walked out, back to his room.

"What the fuck, dude," Swish said as he stormed out of the room.

When I got to work the next day, I had one hell of a black eye. Swish had landed a solid hit, and my eye looked like a black hole.

"Bork!" Sergeant Moore barked.

"Yes, Sarge?" I replied.

"What the fuck happened to your eye?" Sergeant Moore asked.

"I slept wrong, Sarge." I answered. "Nothing to worry about."

"OK, Bork," Sergeant Moore said. "Just don't make me do any paperwork."

"You got it, Sarge." I replied.

As I got to work folding laundry, Officer Smith, a crazy ghetto black woman with a hot body but terrible weave, came out screaming. "Bork! You been fighting, Bork?"

"No, ma'am."

"Don't lie to me, Bork. I see your black eye. I heard you kicked ass and got a win for laundry."

"No, ma'am," I said. "Don't know what you're talking about."

"Miguel! Carlos!" she shouted, sounding batshit crazy. "Did Bork get a win for laundry?"

Carlos smiled and walked away, but Miguel answered.

"Yes, ma'am. Bork whooped ass, literally and metaphorically. Dude tried running away when Bork took off on him, Bork caught him and locked him in the cell with him, choked him out, and left him on the floor."

"Bork!" she screamed with delight. "Way to go, Bork! We finally have a winner in laundry! All the rest of you can't fight, but laundry finally has a winner! If you end up in confinement, I will bail you out 'cause we need more W's in laundry. Don't lose, Bork!"

I just shook my head and went back to folding.

In the dorm the next evening, there was a fight between Snoop and another inmate. I didn't know Snoop's real name either, but that is what everyone called him, because he looked like Snoop Dogg. They were not smart about the fight, these two, as it took place in the dayroom on the second floor, and the officer's station was mere feet away. The officers watched the entire fight, waiting until the end to intervene. There was a bunch of shouting, but it was a struggle for me to understand the Ebonics. With the heat of the fighting, all the other shouting, and the guys hitting each other, I could not make out anything but the occasional "bitch!" and "fuck!"

I was watching this, and I saw Snoop throw the much smaller guy he was fighting. The guy hit the ground at the top of the staircase and rolled—down, down, down the stairs. He got up and had his fists in front of his face, moving them in a jerky manner. Snoop moved to meet him on the stairs, and he grabbed Snoop's legs and slammed Snoop on the floor at the top of the stairs. As they got back to their feet and kept hitting each other, an officer came in and started shouting to break it up or he was going to pepper spray them. They didn't listen and kept fighting, and the officer sprayed them both in the face.

"Everyone on your bunks! Everyone on your bunks!" the officer shouted over the loudspeakers. I headed back to my room as they cuffed up Snoop and the other guy. Before I got out of the dayroom, I saw Swish coming up the stairs, right past the guards who were cuffing the combatants.

We were sitting in our room talking about how the guards saw Swish's black eye as he walked past and discussing what we would say if they came and tried to grab him, thinking that he had been involved in the altercation, when three guards showed up outside our cell door and the door buzzed open.

The guards pulled me and Swish out separately and questioned us in the dayroom. I knew that the limitation on taking us to confinement was forty-eight hours past when the wrongdoing occurred, so Swish and I had already agreed we would tell them the truth about us fighting two days earlier. That's one thing about prison life—you could brawl one day and tell lies together the next. Our black eyes were already changing color, so it was immediately clear that they didn't happen in the last thirty minutes, so it followed that we could not have possibly been involved in the recent scuffle.

As the officers in Florida Department of Corrections were not known for following the rules or being honest, my heart was still pounding in terror at being taken to confinement and losing my gain time. Fortunately, this shift had had enough excitement, and had enough paperwork ahead of them to not want the extra hassle of taking us to confinement too. It also didn't hurt that I'd developed a reputation with the staff for being honest—they took my word regarding what happened and allowed both me and Swish back into our room.

The next day, I saw Chris when he came to laundry to get a bedroll after being released from confinement. I didn't think anything of it until I got back to the dorm in the afternoon—the lock on my locker had been kicked open and my entire canteen had been stolen—not just the canteen, also my shoes, clothing, even my shampoo and deodorant.

I asked everyone on my wing of the dorm if they'd seen who came in, because my wing was all old convicts, guys who'd been locked up for ten years or more, and they had a code, honor amongst thieves if you will. Everyone on that wing had plenty of canteen too, and no reason to steal. Besides, I'd earned their respect for being clean, doing good business, and not bringing attention or chaos into the area. Generally, these guys didn't to snitch, but there were ways around that. Josh and Tony both told me that they'd been on the wing all day, and the only outsider who passed through was my former roommate Chris. That was a no-snitching way of telling me that he was the one who robbed me.

I didn't want to believe Chris would steal from me.

I went to the elderly officer in the station, told her what had happened, and asked her if she could roll back the cameras so that I could see who went into my room. Unfortunately, the only person who even approached my room that day was Chris. The officer asked me if I wanted to have her call down to the other end of the compound and have them search his stuff, and I agreed. About ten minutes later, she told me that Chris admitted that he stole my stuff and had already traded it for drops of acid. She also told me that he must have dropped the acid already as they found no signs of contraband on him.

I got it. They couldn't help me, but they respected me just enough to let me know that he was guilty, and the next move was mine.

I went back to my room and thought things through. The next day, Chris would be on the schedule to go to Classification to receive his new job assignment. He'd have to walk right past laundry to get there, and he'd have to walk past it again after Classification to go back to his dorm.

Everyone around me expected that I would handle this with violence.

I slept on it.

The next morning when I was working in laundry, I heard, "Count clear," and knew there'd be open movement on the compound in just minutes.

"Hey!" I shouted to Sergeant Moore. "Can you open the gate for me? I need to go get the laundry from medical."

"Sure, Bork." Sergeant Moore walked out of laundry and toward the gate that gave access to the back road running end to end on the compound.

I followed behind Chris—the timing was perfect. Just as Sergeant Moore opened the gate, Chris walked toward me on the back road. As Sergeant Moore turned to walk back to laundry, I made my move.

"Josh, I swear I didn't—"

Thwack! I Superman punched Chris in the jaw with every ounce of force I could muster. His glasses shattered and seemed to explode as he flew six feet across the road and landed in the ditch on the side with a thud. As he tried to get up, I spit in his face.

"I am going to hit you every time I see you," I said. "Until you return every item that you stole from me. Not replacements. Every item, the exact ones you stole. Even if the warden is standing next to you, I am going to knock you out every time I see you."

I turned and walked back to laundry just as Sergeant Moore approached.

"What was that about, Bork?"

"He tripped Sarge," I said. "I tried to be a nice guy and catch him, but I wasn't fast enough."

"Don't make me do paperwork," Moore said, shaking his head as he turned to walk back into laundry.

An hour later, when the call for inmate movement came over the walkie-talkies, I asked Sergeant Moore to open the gate for me.

"Bork," Sergeant Moore repeated, "do not make me do paperwork."

"Sure thing, Sarge," I said, smiling. "Just open the gate and hurry back to laundry. If you don't see it, it didn't happen, and therefore no paperwork."

Sergeant Moore paused for a second, looking at me like I'd said something profound, then proceeded to open the gate and head back to the laundry building. I walked out of the gate and saw Chris coming back from Classification. As he got closer to me, he put his hands up and started blubbering.

"Josh I swear it wasn't—"

Thwack! I Superman punched Chris in the jaw again with every ounce of force I could muster. He flew backward and hit the asphalt with a thud. As he scrambled to get up, I said the exact same thing, but just a little colder: "I am going to hit you every time I see you until you return every item that you stole from me. *Every. Fucking. Time.*"

As I turned around and walked back to laundry, Crause was again walking up, also coming from Classification.

"Daaayum, Bork!" Crause said. "You ain't playing!"

"I don't play about money," I responded.

As I walked back into the laundry building, Sergeant Moore was looking at me reprovingly.

"Don't make me do paperwork, Bork."

"I won't, Sarge," I replied calmly.

In the evening, after shift change, they put cuffs on me.

"Why?"

"No clue," the officer responded. "Captain's orders."

We walked across the compound in the dark together in silence.

I didn't know the captain's name, but she was an older black woman who had always been very professional and didn't harass inmates. When I arrived at her office, most of the lights were off in the building, save for a small lamp on her desk. Seated to the right of her desk was Chris, looking smug.

"Have a seat, inmate Bork," the captain said.

"Yes, ma'am," I replied as I took the seat in front of her desk.

"Do you know why you are here?"

"Well, judging by the fact that Chris is here, I'm assuming it has something to do with all the stuff he stole from me. Did you find my stolen belongings."

"I don't know anything about that," the captain said, looking at Chris with disdain. "This inmate has checked in, saying he fears for his safety from you."

"Yeah!" Chris interrupted, pointing at his jawline. "Look! My face is all swollen from where he hit me!"

"Be quiet, inmate!" the captain said sharply. She pulled out a penlight and shined it on his face. Swelling and lumps were clearly visible.

"I do not see any marks on your face, inmate," she said to Chris. "Inmate Bork, did you strike this inmate today?"

"No, ma'am," I replied. "I was working in laundry all day. Chris is housed on the opposite end of the compound, and I was with Sergeant Moore all day. Please feel free to call him and ask. He will tell you that any kite written by Chris is a lie."

"I believe you, Bork," the captain told me gently. "I have never had an issue with you, and I see you playing in the band. You sound good." She pulled out a walkie-talkie and spoke into it. "Officer Smith, please step back into my office."

As the officer who escorted me here stepped back into her office, the captain said, "Take the cuffs off of Bork, and take this inmate to confinement. Write him a disciplinary report for lying to an officer and abusing the grievance system. Make sure the DR court takes the maximum amount of gain time away, if he even has any to lose, and make sure they put him back out on to the compound after. Make a note that his attempts to check in are to be ignored."

The look of horror that crossed Chris's face was gratifying, and I felt something—it was not quiet joy, but it was a tremendous satisfaction and a feeling of relief that I avoided something terrible. As Officer Smith unlocked my cuffs, I turned my head toward Chris and winked one eye at him. He shuddered in terror and started blubbering to the captain about his jaw and how afraid he was of me once again. I didn't allow myself to smile until I had left the building, but when I did, I must have looked like the Cheshire Cat.

Next day, coming back from laundry, I saw Swift leaving the canteen line with a laundry bag nearly bursting at the seams full of canteen. Sweet! I was going to get paid.

I followed him into the dorm and caught up to him as he was walking toward his room with the humongous bag of canteen. He currently owed me about a hundred dollars, the equivalent of $10,000 out on the street. I'd never had an issue with him paying me before, so I wasn't expecting any pushback when I went to collect. His family sent him money every month, and he went to the canteen line once per month and paid back all his debts first.

"Hey, Swift!" I called. "Glad you finally hit the window. I can take that off your hands and clear your debt."

"No, man, sorry," Swift said. "You have to wait till next month. I have to pay off Twitch's debt, because he's supposed to go home in sixty days, but he owes so much money for drugs that he won't make it that long without my help."

"I'm sorry to hear that," I said. "But that's not my problem. My problem is the money that you owe me that you're giving to someone else instead. You need to tell him to handle his own debts. Otherwise, *you* might not make it home."

"You wanna fight about it?" Swift asked.

"You know I don't have a choice," I responded. "You owe me a four-week-old debt that's not insignificant. You're going to have fight me in order to buy yourself another month."

"Then that's what I'll have to do," Swift said as he took off his shirt.

I was further into the room than he was, and as soon as he took off his shirt, he dropped his head and shoulders and charged me.

One of the first things I ever learned in martial arts was that the easiest way to defeat a charging opponent was to simply step out of their way, much like a matador and a bull. Although the distance was not great, only about five feet, I stepped backward and around with my left foot, pivoting on my right and allowing him to pass as I turned to keep my body facing him. I grabbed him by his pants with my right hand and by the back of the neck with my left hand, amplifying his charge as I spun him in a circle until his momentum came to a sudden stop when his head collided with the solid concrete wall behind me.

He hit with such momentum that his whole body bounced off the wall. I turned with him, not letting go of the back of his pants or the back of his neck. As his bounce came to a stop, I changed direction and yanked him back around counterclockwise as hard as I could, slamming his head into the block wall a second time. He bounced off the wall a second time, and I repeated the process once more.

The third time I bounced his head off of the concrete block wall, his roommate standing in the door watching said, "That's enough, Bork. Let him fight."

I let go of his pants with my right hand, grabbing his left wrist and pulling it around to the small of his back. I let go of his neck with my left hand and reached it under his left arm to grab my right wrist. In Brazilian jujitsu, this technique is called a Kimura. Since his head was next to my hip and his shoulder near my pelvis, he attempted to grab under my leg and scoop me to body slam me. Unfortunately for him, I'd done this dance once or twice, and I was already jumping up in order to get both of my legs around his waist, while I cranked his hand behind his back up toward his head. He kept trying to stand up, but he couldn't, so he started pinching me. Yes, pinching. What the hell, was I back in kindergarten?

Since his shoulder was by my face, I opened my mouth as wide as I could and bit down on the flesh of his shoulder blade *hard*. I felt his skin break, and the coppery taste of warm, wet blood flooded my mouth. He screamed, but he didn't stop fighting, so I twisted my body and shifted my weight to the side, yanking his wrist toward the back of his head as hard as I could. There was a pop as his shoulder dislocated, and it was so loud that it scared me into letting go. He stumbled backward, blood dripping down his back, his arm dangling in an unnatural fashion.

"What the hell, man!" he said in disgust. "You fucking bit me!"

"Yes," I replied. "That's one of the reasons why Marines are called devil dogs. We bite like a bitch!"

As I walked out of the room past him, I said, "You've got one month to get me my money."

But over the next few weeks, I started to feel regret for what I had done to Swift. He was able to get someone to help him get his arm relocated, but the spot where I bit him got infected and started to fester and ooze. He also started to develop noticeable memory, mood, and personality changes. I was thinking I may have caused a traumatic brain injury—and the guy was only a few months away from going home.

A few weeks later, he came into my room and dumped a bag of canteen on my bunk.

"We good?" he asked.

I counted through it.

"Yeah," I replied. "We're good. Sorry about the shoulder."

"Nah," Swift said. "I had it coming. I should have paid you. I just couldn't let Twitch get killed, and I knew you would hurt me but not kill me. Better option."

Fuck. Now I felt even worse. He chose self-sacrifice to help his druggie friend? I was the asshole. *Fuck.* I was such a scumbag.

Maybe I was done being the storeman.

I didn't want to hurt anyone anymore.

Fuck!

The days rolled on. When I wasn't in the chapel with the band or working or reading or hustling, I played Dungeons & Dragons with my nerd kinship, and it was good—anything to escape the horrors of prison.

We made a funny group of fantasy role-players: Shane Runkle, Samuel Keller, Swift, and Solo.

Shane was a Marine Corps veteran who looked like Edward Norton and had a blindingly sharp intellect and dry sense of humor to match. He had a life sentence for a home invasion—the homeowner had come home in the while Shane was making off with a TV and some jewelry, tried to wrestle Shane, and got a broken nose for his stupid decision. Shane had been locked up since the 1990s.

Samuel Keller was a young, balding white kid with Harry Potter glasses, in his twenties, who had been locked up for nearly ten years, and would tactfully avoid telling you why he was locked up regardless of how hard you pried, which usually meant a sex offense, but if he wasn't flaunting, I was not prying. He was rather annoying, in the way that a nerdy outcast at the reject table in high school who suffered from a serious case of arrogance could be annoying, but he could hold an intelligent conversation, and he was a good gamer.

Swift was, of course, one of my best customers. He was goofy, maybe five feet tall, clearly not old enough to drink, had mild anger management issues, and was seriously into D&D—like, so into it that he probably needed an intervention.

Solo was a white guy, dark-haired, twenty-eight just like me, covered in crappy prison tattoos, an orthodox Jew, and a member of the Folk Nation gang. He had a razor-sharp wit, and he was usually saying something sarcastic and condescending.

Together, we played two campaigns. Shane was dungeon master for the "Rise of the Rune Lords," an amazing goblin-focused adventure. I was the dungeon master for my own game, one that came straight from my imagination—the guys were enraptured. We played Shane's game every Monday and Thursday for about three hours after work, and we played my game Tuesday, Wednesday, and Friday for about three hours, and Saturday and Sunday for about eight hours each day.

Life carried on, but after being robbed for everything in my locker, it was very difficult to operate a store. I needed money to loan in order to make money. I decided that I needed to go on a collecting spree, especially as I had some debts that were nearing the four-week mark.

I looked to the oldest debts first, and I saw that Christopher owed me a substantial amount—he had hit me up a bunch of times in the first two weeks and paid just enough to show me he intended to pay. It was a little like paying the minimum on a maxed-out credit card, only more dangerous and with much higher interest.

I searched the dorm to find him—he was smoking with JC.

"Hey, man," I said, "you owe me a lot of money, and I need you to pay up. Been four weeks, and I really cannot wait any longer. What can you come up with right now?"

"I don't have shit." he said. "I ain't paying you nothing. If you have a problem with that, get it in blood."

"OK then," I said flatly. "Tighten up. But heads up—if knock you out, I am going to rape you."

JC straightened up a little and said, "Not here. Too much traffic, too much heat."

"My room," I said and backed out, keeping my eyes on him.

When we got to my room, JC pulled the door shut, flipped the foot of Swish's mattress up, and jumped up to sit on the steel top bunk for a front-row seat.

"I closed the door to keep prying eyes away" he says. "Guys ready? Fight!"

As I turned my head from JC to Christopher, I got caught off guard. Christopher was already throwing a wild haymaker with his right hand. No time to do anything but drop my chin—his fist slammed into my forehead. I think he split the skin above my eyebrow.

When he threw the next one, I dropped my weight and shot in for his legs like a wrestler. I scooped under him, lifting him up. As I drove forward and began to slam him down, I panicked because I saw the stainless steel toilet behind him, and I imagined his head hitting it, breaking his neck and getting me a murder charge. I dropped him with the steel toilet landing dead on the center of his spine—crack!— but I wasn't sure if it was his back or the toilet.

I backed up, to get as far away from the danger zone as possible in a confined space, as he rolled off the toilet and got up. He charged me, and I clinched up with him, using his momentum to slam him into the wall. I yanked his head down and then started slamming my knee into his stomach and chest, over and over again. By the third time, he was no longer fighting back, but he hadn't quit either. He was trying to block the knees, but his forearms couldn't take anymore, and he just covered his face with his arms while I kept driving my knee into his torso, again and again, I was surprised that he was still standing, but hitting him was like hitting a tree trunk.

I have this odd habit of counting my strikes when I fight. I think it's connected to my OCD, like having to count every toothbrush stroke or wash your hands an exact number of times. Anyway, I hit Christopher in the chest with my knees exactly thirty-seven times when he started coughing up blood, and another twelve times before JC jumped off the bunk and pushed us apart.

"That's enough," he said. "You're done. Break it up."

As I backed up, I realized that the white walls of my room were bright red and pink, covered in blood. The ceiling had blood all over it, as did the floor, my shirt, and my pants. For a moment, I thought I was a badass, till I realized that at least half of the blood was from the cut on my forehead.

JC took off his shirt and used it to wipe Chris down so that he didn't appear to have bathed in blood as he walked across the dorm to his room. Chris was swaying on his feet, blood bubbling from his mouth and nose with every labored breath.

"I'll be back to help you clean up," JC said. "Let me make sure he gets back to his room and doesn't die walking down the stairs."

As he escorted Chris out of my room and down the hall, Swish walked in and stopped dead in his tracks.

"What. The. Fuck. Did you murder someone in here? It looks like a slaughterhouse."

Swish grabbed his dirty uniform pants and started wiping the blood off of the walls as I used his towel to wipe the opposite wall.

"Hey!" Swish said. "That's my towel, yo!"

"I work in laundry, dumbass. I'll bring you a brand-new one tomorrow."

"OK," Swish said. "At least, you didn't get any blood on my mattress. How did you manage that?"

"Very carefully."

A few minutes later as we were finishing cleaning the last of the blood off the ceiling, JC came back.

"You good, kid?" he asked me.

"Yeah, man. I'm fine," I responded. "Just a scratch on my forehead."

"You know why I was in here with you?" JC asked me.

"Actually, I don't," I said. "I was wondering why a white supremacist was mediating a fight between a Jew and a black. Care to enlighten me?"

"Look," JC said, "we are supposed to hate Jews, ideologically. But the truth is, we don't hate Jews. Jews are good at business and don't bother anyone. Jews make for good scapegoats, but *really* we hate blacks. They're dirty, dishonest, ignorant, violent, smelly, and generally unpleasant to be around."

"All right, all right," I said, trying to get him past it. "But that doesn't explain why you were in here mediating a fight between us. Seems to me you'd want us to kill each other. Solves your problem for you."

"True," JC said. "However, I like *you*. You are honest, clean, good business, and you are a military veteran. You don't belong here. The world could use more people like you. I was here to make sure *you* didn't kill *him*, 'cause you deserve to go home."

That stunned me.

Never for a second had I even considered that he had been there to protect me. I'm a Jew—once an orthodox Jew, who wore tzitzit and a yarmulke, prayed three times a day, and observed the Sabbath to the letter. A white supremacist with a giant swastika on his head was volunteering to protect me?

I already regularly felt like Alice after she fell down the rabbit hole, but this was weird beyond Wonderland.

One day, a new busload of inmates arrived. I knew the first thing that many of them were going to do was ask who the storeman was, as they'd have to wait a few days before their canteen account balances caught up to them. They were limited in how much they could bring with them as they were transferred from place to place, so they would need to stock up on basic things.

As I expected, immediately upon entering the dorm, a couple of the new guys could be heard shouting, "Hey! Who's the storeman here?"

I stepped out to the dayroom and responded, "That would be me. What you need?"

I could see the look of excitement on the faces of the new inmates when they realized that the storeman was a young white boy. The excitement was predatory, and their body language was easy to decipher. The shoulders hunched forward, the hands being rubbed together just like a Disney villain about to do something bad and expecting to get away with it.

"Yo!" one of the old black men playing chess in the dayroom said as he touched the arm of an all-too-eager inmate. "Don't go borrowing from that white boy unless you plan on paying him."

Maybe he thought I couldn't hear him, or maybe he didn't care. Either way, the new inmate shrugged off the old man and his warning. "Why? He's a white boy. He can't fight. Easy pickings."

The old man looked up at the new guy with a grim look on his face. "That's the wrong white boy. He can fight, he don't care who you is or where you is, and he gonna fuck you in the ass if you lose. Don't go fucking wit' him unless you plan to pay. He a crash dummy."

Suddenly, the new inmate had other things to do.

As I went about my business, I started noticing that when I overheard conversations about myself, that crazy term kept coming up. Crash Dummy.

I could live with it.

In fact, I smiled every time I heard it.

VET DORMS
AND BIG STORMS

In September of 2017, one of the largest storms of my adult life hit Florida. Hurricane Irma had been all over the news for days. They kept expecting it to go one way, then another. Having spent most of my life in Florida, I don't even worry about a storm until it's a Category 5. Anything less and it's beach weather. Most Floridians feel this way too, so that, despite the strange weather of the day, despite the wind really been picking up, and despite the local news that we were allowed to see and their scare tactics, none of us were paying any attention—not the inmates, not the guards. Business as usual:

Dungeons & Dragons with Shane, Solo, and the guys, working out on the rec yard, reading books, a regular day.

And then all of the loudspeakers on the compound kicked on.

"Yard closed. Yard closed. Return to your dorms. Yard closed."

In the middle of rec? I figured something must have happened on the other end of the compound. They locked us down anytime there was any altercation, even one that had nothing to do with us. Maybe it was a scuffle because of all of the new inmates transferred over from other, more violent locations.

Grudgingly everyone on the yard complied, heading back to our dorms. A few of the inmates who had "special" relationships with one or another of the officers schmoozed for a few extra minutes while everyone else was trickling back into the dorms. The guards came in last, and only then did they tell us that we were on lockdown because of the hurricane. The wind had rattled the perimeter fence so bad that it triggered an alarm—as if there were an inmate climbing it. The fences were not electric like the kind in movies—you wouldn't get shocked if you touched them—but they did have sensors that registered motion for anything larger than a small bird. Now the heavy gusts we were getting was generating so many false alarms that they *had* to lock us down to make sure no one used this weather as an opportunity to escape.

We were locked in, but we still had the freedom to wander around the dorm. The T-buildings were designed for higher security than the open-bay dorms, with concrete roofs, concrete walls two stories tall, and tiny jalousie windows with bars. Very hurricane proof.

The open-bay dorms, on the other hand, had shingle roofs, lots of windows, and were only one story, so if there was a storm surge all the inmates would die.

Not long after we were locked in, we were ordered to our bunks. We got locked in, and then they started bringing in all the inmates from the open-bay dorms, three grown men to a six-by-eight-foot room, roughly forty-eight square feet with a steel toilet and bunk beds occupying most of that space.

This was not cool.

As it turned out, I wasn't the only person who thought this wasn't a good idea.

Every single person in the dorm was upset, but especially the guys with life sentences. Once all the rooms had three men, the guards closed the steel gates to each wing of the dorm and unlocked our individual rooms. At least, we had a hallway we could roam in, since it's not that fun to poop with two grown men sitting inches away watching you.

This madness was how we enjoyed the rest of the day, although it was excruciatingly warm. Florida prisons don't have air-conditioning, and only the open-bay dorms had fans. The dorms that had cells had a fan in the dayroom, but nothing in the hallways or rooms where we stayed. Whatever the temperature was outside during Florida summers, it was fifteen degrees warmer inside, at times so hot that the walls, concrete block walls, actually sweat. These walls had been painted with latex, and when they started sweating, pockets of moisture ballooned out in the paint until someone couldn't help themselves and popped it, releasing up to a few gallons of water at once. With three men in a forty-eight-square-foot room, multiplied by 120 rooms, the heat and humidity was truly stifling. Every time one of us took our shirt off to cope with the heat, the officers came on the loudspeakers ordering us to put our full uniform back on. The full uniform was boxers, shorts, pants, undershirt, overshirt, socks, and crocks. In Florida. In the hottest month of the year. While it was ninety-nine-plus degrees outside, 115–125 inside, 100 percent humidity, with 360 sweaty men, latex paint, and poor ventilation.

Yeah, this was going to turn out wonderfully.

Within an hour, there were three fights just on one floor of the dorm. We couldn't see who was fighting, because they had us segregated from the wing, but we could hear them. After the third fight, we were ordered to our rooms and locked in. If you thought it was miserable before being locked in, this was next level. Now I couldn't even watch the storm 'cause there were no windows.

When dinnertime came, there was no call for chow. The doors were not opened, and the shouting from the inmates began. Eventually, hours after we were supposed to eat, three officers and three kitchen inmates showed up on the wing and started passing out food.

"A peanut butter sandwich?" someone shouted. "You gotta be kidding me! It is not even raining, and you have us crammed in here like sardines. What the fuck yo!"

When they got to my room, it did turn out to be nothing but a glob of peanut butter between two stale pieces of Wonderbread and a Styrofoam cup with warm water in it.

"Seriously?" I asked. "You give us stale bread, a glob of peanut butter, and not enough water to prevent choking. Can I have a second cup of water, please?"

The inmate passing out the food and water shook his head and kept moving on. Luckily for me, one of the other inmates passing out the food was on the praise band with me, so when the officer was distracted, he gave me a second cup and swiped an apple from one of the bags set aside for people with AIDS, as they somehow got four thousand calories per day instead of the twelve hundred the rest of us got. I hid the apple under my pillow so the officer wouldn't see it, and waited until they had left to start eating my food. I wanted to put some of the peanut butter on my apple, because that was a luxury I hadn't had in four years.

As the evening turned into night, the gusts of wind became stronger and more constant. It wasn't raining during the day, but it started raining sporadically as the evening continued. The inmate who was sharing the room with us was lying on the floor, and as the wind picked up and the rain started falling more horizontally, he started getting wet.

"Shut the fucking window, man!" he said.

Swish and I looked at each other, then looked at him at the same time.

"It is over a hundred degrees in here at 9:00 p.m.," I said. "This window is our only ventilation, our only fresh air, and our air-conditioning. It stays open. Go lay by the toilet if you want to stay dry."

"What the fuck did you just say to me?"

Swish leaned forward from where he was sitting on his bunk and placed a hand on my shoulder to stop me from reacting.

"Hey, guy," Swish said. "This is our room. You are a guest in our house. We do what we want in our house, and if you don't like it, you can leave."

"How the fuck am I supposed to leave? I don't want to be here any more than you want me here. Close the window."

"You know who he is, right?" Swish said. "I suggest you simmer down before you get hurt and I have to watch you get raped. If you keep going, you and Josh are going to fight. If Josh knocks you out, he is going to rape you. Is that a chance you're willing to take? If not, the window stays open."

Our guest clenched his fists a few times, and I could see the wheel turning in his head. He was trying to decide if he believed the rumors about me being a crash dummy, and about me raping anyone I knocked out. He was trying to decide if the risk was worth getting his way. If this was a cartoon, there would be smoke coming from his ears and an X-ray cutaway of his brain showing the mouse peddling frantically on the bike that was powering the brain, and then the lightbulb finally came on.

"Fine," our guest said. "Leave it open."

As the night went on, the wind started howling. All three of us started watching through the window. The bench on the side of the basketball court got ripped in half and flew away. The megaphone bolted to the side of the building came off, but slowly, one bolt at a time. We took bets on which gust was going to take it all the way off. Swish was cheering for it to hang in there and not give up. I was rooting for the wind to destroy the prison. Our guest didn't choose a side.

In the middle of the night, the power went out. What little ventilation we had in the form of a central fan for the entire building died. The heat almost instantly became twice as bad. We had a puddle of water on the floor from all the rain coming in, and the rain was constant now. The lights all over the compound went out and the generator kicked in a few minutes later, then died too. A portion of the fence got ripped away, I think. It was really hard to tell in the dark with the wind and the rain through a tiny window.

A miserable night—I finally fell asleep as the bricks let go of the daytime heat, and the dorm cooled to the upper nineties. Sometime in the morning, the storm abated, and there was just some light wind and lots of sun. The heat started cranking up as the sun turned all the moisture into a sauna.

For the next fourteen days, we were confined to this room. It didn't make sense, since the weather was beautiful. We got the same meal for breakfast, lunch, and dinner, fourteen days straight. Peanut butter, stale bread, and a small cup of water. And we were dehydrated—chapped lips, dry mouth, dizziness—and constipation. It was agony. It took two weeks before they got the power back on, and without the central air, there was absolutely zero ventilation. Grown men were screaming out of the windows to the officers, begging for water, begging for air, threatening suicide just to get out of the dorm into the ninety-eight-degree sunlight outside the dorm. Far as I know, they never did get the generator back up and running.

I later learned that the eye of the storm had passed directly over us, causing widespread damage. They would not let us out of the dorms until the fence was repaired and the power grid and security system were fully functional. When they grid came back online, there were thunderous cheers coming from the nearly four hundred men in this tiny dorm, and we could hear the cheers from the other dorms hundreds of yards away. The central fan kicked back in, and the ice-cold ninety-eight-degree outside air started getting sucked in through the window. Praise be to God for this! It felt like the coldest air-conditioning I had ever felt in my life!

The first chance we got to leave the dorm, everyone looked like survivors coming out from an underground bunker to bear witness to a dystopian apocalypse. Everyone was moving slow, looking around as if seeing their surroundings for the first time, taking a moment to just feel the sun on their faces and the ninety-eight-degree cool breeze brushing their skin. If I had not been experiencing the same sense of wonder as everyone else, I would have been laughing because of how comical we must have appeared.

After a few weeks, life went back to normal. For most of us, that meant falling into the same routine of chow, rec yard, TV, sleep. For me, I had never in my life been so excited to play Dungeons & Dragons or take a shower. This feeling was short-lived, however, as the building on the opposite end of the compound, fox dorm, suffered more damage than the echo dorm had. In response to the additional damage, the administration decided to make fox dormitory the "veteran and honor dorm." In layman's terms, this meant they were going to fill the place with all the inmates who wouldn't complain about being in a building that should have been condemned.

I rolled up my mattress, packed up all of my belongings, and made my way to the other end of the compound. As I got into my dorm, it appeared to be exactly the same as echo dorm. The only major difference was that the windows were smaller, couldn't be opened or closed, and allowed for less ventilation.

I found myself fortunate that there were few enough veterans on the compound to ensure that we each had our own room. Most of the veterans that were moved here were unhappy about being moved, because most of the veterans were lifers who had been living in the same dorm with the same inmates for twenty to fifty years. This change was uncomfortable for them, and exposed them to inmates that were much younger, and had much less time, thereby removing the small bubble of peace that they had created for themselves.

As it turned out, there were not enough inmates that had been discipline-free for two years or more in order to make this a full-scale honor dorm. There was also no interest in being in the honor dorm because the administration assigned the worst officers on the compound to the place without providing any actual incentive to justify why this dorm should be better for those who have served in the military or stayed out of trouble during their time in prison. Their talk of getting flat-screen TVs, of being the first dorm to go to chow, of getting priority for the canteen line was just that—talk. It never came to fruition. The one positive part of being there was that it was very quiet on the veteran's wing, and I was the youngest person there by at least twenty years. Of all the places I could be forced to finish my remaining time, this was not the worst place to be.

Once the officers realized that they were not going to have any problems with the veterans and the inmates in the veterans' honor dorm, they chilled out. For the most part, they left us alone and recognized that there was really nothing that made this dorm better than any other dorm. The officers acknowledged that we all got a crappy deal, as the foundation of the building was separating from the walls, allowing water and an extraordinary large number of cockroaches into the dormitory. Half of the plumbing in the building didn't work, the vacuum breakers in the stainless steel toilets were old, and oftentimes when we flushed the toilets, the toilets would stay running like a vortex for hours until the work order got put in and the maintenance inmates could come out and work on it.

The guards that were assigned to the veteran/honor dorm were all as laid-back as any I had encountered during my entire stay—with one exception. Her name was Officer Free. She was a dirty blond officer in her twenties, slender, and not terribly unattractive. She had a prosthetic leg and a foul attitude, and on the shifts when she worked, she came in and took down the bedsheet that we used as a shower curtain. I'm not sure why she wanted two hundred grown men to look at each other while they showered, as it didn't pose a security risk since the shower itself was already outside the line of sight of the officer station.

One thing was for certain about prisoners: we were creative. We took a piece of a trash bag, and we tied it to the middle of a pen on one end and to a cell bar on the other end. We spun the pen round and round, so the plastic of the trash bag turned into a braid and stretched while braiding. We did this a few times and created a couple of plastic strings, which we then used as shower curtain rings, and tied another bedsheet to the entrance of the shower. Figuring that was the end of that, we went back to taking showers as normal with a curtain to give us privacy. It was all well and good until the next time Officer Free was assigned to the veteran dorm.

"Everyone outside your cells!" Officer Free shouted. "Inspection!"

As we all stood in front of our cells with our hands behind our back, the warden and assistant warden came through for cell inspections. They didn't really bother us as we were all veterans, and our beds were made, rooms clean, and they didn't have any problems with us. However, after the warden and assistant warden moved on to another wing, Officer Free came back and pulled out a knife. She tried to cut the shower curtain down with the knife, but our ingenuity was too much for her, and she found herself unable to cut through the plastic strings. She got mad, pulled out her lighter, and set the entire shower curtain on fire!

"That'll teach you," she grunted through gritted teeth as the bedsheet curtain caught fire.

"Is that really necessary?" Trueblood, a Vietnam veteran, asked.

"Yes, it is," Officer Free said aggressively, with the lighter in one hand and the drawn knife in the other hand. "You are not allowed to have a curtain."

Trueblood went back into his room, just shaking his head.

God, I thought, *I will be so happy to get out of here and go home.*

As my days here started to wind to a close, I started talking to my dad every weekend on the phone. He was my release address, though he wouldn't let me come stay with him because I didn't have a good relationship with my stepmom. We started discussing probation and employment, and my dad took it upon himself to pay all of the fines and fees associated with state probation so that I could leave prison and deal with federal probation.

When the altercation with the officer occurred, I was terrified that I was going to spend the rest of my life in prison. Even though it was just a broken nose, the jail had the police enhance my charge from battery to aggravated battery, which, in any other state, requires permanent disfigurement or severe bodily harm. Only here was a broken nose considered permanent disfigurement *and* severe bodily harm. Additionally, although the officer was off-duty and just there to pick up a paycheck, the jail had the police enhance the severity of my charge by including law enforcement officer in the description. So instead of simple battery, the charge got upgraded to aggravated battery, and then upgraded again to aggravated battery on a law enforcement officer. This was a charge that was a first-degree felony of the same severity as homicide and rape. I was only twenty-five years old, facing the very real possibility that I could spend thirty years in prison—that is, if I survived that long.

Week after week, I sent my father panicked letters requesting a lawyer. The public defender had no interest in defending me. In fact, the public defender's office was directly across the hall from the prosecutor's office, and they were fishing buddies. Week after week, I told my father the same story about what happened, about how my altercation with the correctional officer was entirely self-defense. Week after week, I told my father about the abuse I was suffering; about being starved, beaten, pepper sprayed, and forced to eat and drink sewage from the toilet for the officer's entertainment.

Not once did I receive any response from Dad. It was as if I never existed.

I knew there had to be video footage of the events that transpired. There were two high-resolution, color cameras in the jail that recorded twenty-four seven. I told my public defender that the video footage would exonerate me, or at least reduce my charge to something that carried a maximum of five years instead of a minimum of five years and a maximum of thirtyu years. A violent charge of aggravated battery on a law enforcement officer is significantly worse than simple battery as a result of self-defense. Had this happened in a metropolitan area like Miami, Orlando, New York, or Chicago, I would have gotten a slap on the wrist. Probation at worst. But because this took place in a white, country, small town, they wanted to bury me. I was the wrong kind of white. I wasn't a meth-addicted, white supremacist, Southern Baptist Klansman.

The jail and the prosecutor's office resisted providing copies of the video footage to my attorney. When my attorney finally received video footage, it had been edited to only show the segment where I was hitting the correctional officer. My attorney never received the portion of the footage immediately before the violence that would have clearly identified my reactions as self-defense, and my attorney never received the portion of the footage immediately after the violence that showed the extreme abuse I endured at the hands of the officers.

I had originally been arrested for conspiracy to commit fraud, and most people don't understand what that means. Hell, I didn't understand what that meant. Most people, such as my father, assume that being arrested for a crime is the same as being convicted of a crime, because police officers are perfect and they wouldn't arrest you if you weren't doing something wrong, and most people also assume that conspiracy to commit a crime is the same as committing a crime.

This is not so.

However, since I had been arrested for conspiracy to commit fraud, my father made the normal assumption that I was dishonest and anything I said was questionable at best. My father dismissed all of my complaints of the abuse that I was suffering as a form of manipulation or an attempt to play the victim. He washed his hands of me as a lost cause and cut all ties. It would be two and a half years before my father and I had interaction again, and then not because he had a sudden change of heart regarding my innocence.

Nearly four years and eight months into my sentence, a DVD containing the entire footage of the event arrived in my father's mailbox—less than four weeks before the end of my sentence, when I was to be released. The last year of my incarceration, my father, and I had reconnected and were speaking on the telephone for fifteen minutes every Saturday. When he realized that I was going to make it to the end without getting more time added, he decided that he was willing to start speaking to me again. I would likely show up on his doorstep the day I was released anyway. Might as well be on his terms. The Saturday immediately following the arrival of the DVD, my father mentioned that it had arrived and that he had taken the time to watch it.

"Joshua," he said, "I owe you an apology. The DVD arrived this week, and I watched it. I'm sorry I didn't believe you when you told me that you broke the officer's nose in self-defense. For the past five years, your story of the events that transpired have never wavered. You've told the same story for five years straight, and the video footage on the DVD matched your story perfectly. If I had seen this video footage five years ago, I would have gotten you the best attorney money could buy. I'm so sorry that I could have prevented your five years in prison. If only I had believed you."

"Dad," I replied, "all the signs of truth were there. A lie changes a little with every telling. Gets a little bigger, a little more polished. That's how you catch someone lying, because the devil is in the details. The first clue that I was telling you the truth was that in five years, my narrative of the events that transpired never changed, not once. Not a single detail."

As I said this to my father, my voice was soft. I was sitting on the floor in the phone room with my back against the concrete wall. I was keeping my eyes on the other inmates who were there speaking to their families, to make sure that any potential signs of emotion or vulnerability were not picked up or witnessed by anyone else.

"You are right," Dad said. I could hear weary resignation in his voice, bordering on sorrow.

"Moreover," I said, "even if I was lying, what parent doesn't know the sound of real pain in their child's voice? Even if I was lying, or at the very least exaggerating, you should have been able to see, hear and feel the level of distress that I was experiencing and recognize it as real." I was fighting back tears, because this was the first time that Dad had ever admitted that I was right or, more importantly, that he had made a mistake. I felt a connection to my father unlike anything I had previously felt with him, despite being on a phone inside prison.

"You are right, Josh," Dad replied softly.

"Telling me I am right doesn't do anything to fix what has happened," I said, my voice tight with the acute pain of finally being heard. "Being right doesn't undo what has been done to me. Being right doesn't make me feel loved or protected. I don't care about being right because it doesn't change anything."

"I am sorry, Josh," Dad said, the sadness and fatigue in his voice tangible even over the phone. I think he may have been crying, because his voice wavered in a way I had never heard.

"While I appreciate the apology," I replied, pausing to control my breathing and prevent tears from flowing, "it also doesn't change anything. What I care about is that you believe me, trust me, or simply care enough about me to humor me when I reach out for support. I have never asked you for money, cars, or for you to do anything risky or unethical. You're my dad, and the one person who should always be there for me when I am hurting or not strong enough to handle something alone. You are supposed to be my advocate, my friend, my mentor, and my pillar of strength. You were nowhere to be found when I needed you most. How could you? Next time, don't turn your back on me even if you don't believe me."

"That's fair," Dad said, his voice cracking under the agony of having failed his only son. "I love you, Josh."

"I love you too, Dad," I whispered as I hung up the phone. One tear slipped down my face, and I wiped it away as fast as I could, hoping that no one had seen it.

I found that the days, weeks, and months all slowed down to a standstill. The closer I got to going home, the longer each day was. The closer I got to going home, the more everything about being here bothered me.

The black men who sat in the dayroom masturbating every time any female officer was in the officer station disgusted me now more than it used to. Before, I would just shake my head and ignore it, but now it made my blood boil. That woman was someone's mother, sister, wife, or daughter. "Gunning"—what the black inmates call masturbating in front of an unwilling or unknowing person—is predatory.

The inmates who thought they were the next rap superstar were infuriating, with their nose against a wall, beating on their chest or a window or a door to create a bass rhythm, forcing everybody else to listen to them, when they had no talent and used the exact same beat every time.

The officers with their holier-than-thou attitudes, treating us like we are less than animals.

Being forced to eat my food in the chow hall so fast that I got indigestion every time. Making me throw my food away if I tried to have a conversation with somebody at the table, because talking means you're done eating.

The smell every time I walked past a room where two men just finished having anal sex, using mayonnaise as lubricant.

Every perceived slight. Every bit of disrespect. I wanted to fight everybody.

Things that never used to bother me were now worthy of sending somebody to the hospital. The closer I got to going home, the more scared I became of how big of a change it was going to be, while at the same time being terrified that any misstep could stop me from going home, and force me to remain in this hellhole.

Everyone who had previously served time talked about the last six months being the hardest. It never made any sense to me, and it seemed incomprehensible that after years of learning how to survive and getting into a routine, that you would wake up one morning and—*boom!*—everything falls apart because you dropped under six months till freedom.

It was incomprehensible until the day I woke up, six months before going home. Something was different. Noises were louder. Smells were more putrid. The spoiled food tasted fouler. The humid air was more oppressive. Suddenly, I understood.

Everything irritated me because I was afraid, and fear manifests as anger when you live in a place where showing fear is weakness that can get you killed, or worse.

It has taken me years to admit and understand this, but I was afraid of all the things that could go wrong during the next six months. All the things that could extend my stay and prevent me from being free.

Misery loves company, and on the inside, the blacks openly hate the whites. Rarely was an opportunity to hurt a white guy missed. If those individuals knew that you were getting close to going home, they would stop at nothing to prevent it. There were guys who would go out of their way to get you in trouble, whether directly picking fights and using violence, or indirectly by setting you up and snitching to the officers, such as putting a cell phone or drugs under your pillow while you were at work and telling the officer that it was there.

In addition to the problems that other inmates could create for you, there were the problems that the officers could create. If you were to politely say, "Good morning, ma'am," to a female officer who was having a bad day or was just on a power trip, she could throw you in confinement for sexual harassment and extend your sentence, or simply say you touched her, which would add two serious charges (sexual battery *and* battery on a law enforcement officer). There would be no proof needed because her word would suffice. There were dozens of guys I encountered who had served five years or more because of this when their original prison sentence was less than two years. Terrifying.

The fear was not just about the things that could happen before going home, though. The fear *of* going home was horrible. Why would anyone be afraid *of* going home? For starters, Florida has a 97 percent recidivism rate because the system is designed to make sure you fail. The prison industry is Florida's largest revenue producer, generating more income for the state than even the tourism industry. Ensuring that you return is just good business. The things that make sure you return are the restitution, which you *must start paying immediately upon release*, the inability to get housing without a job, and the inability to get a job without permanent housing. Further, few in Florida will rent to anyone with a criminal record, and the only industries who hire convicted felons in Florida are the restaurant and the construction industries, neither of which have living wages at entry level.

The fear of failure, of *coming back to prison,* was overwhelming. It consumed most of my waking hours and kept me wide awake at night too. I was going to be starting over, with a fove-year gap in employment history, in housing history, an expired driver's license, no vehicle, no clothing or possessions other than the outfit they gave me to go home in. I was going to have to explain to every potential employer why I had a five-year gap, reliving this hell over and over, facing rejection over and over, after I had already spent five years paying my debt to society. Then I was going to have to experience the same thing every place I applied for housing. I was terrified that I would be judged, found a failure before I even had a chance to prove myself, and would land right back here. I would let my dad down, and if I came back a second time would be even more alone than I had been this time.

Finally, underneath all that fear was something else. Something even deeper and more sinister. Shame. I was ashamed that I was going home. I was ashamed that I was going home and the people around me were not. That I would leave this place and potentially have something better while they remained here in hell, suffering and miserable. Shane had a life sentence. He would never see freedom. Justin and Trueblood would never see freedom. I felt guilty that I was leaving and these men who had been kind to me, who had made much of this horror more bearable, who had been family to me for the last few years. It was a deep sadness to know that Shane had already been here for nearly thirty years, and that Trueblood had been here for even longer, and that as gentle and kind as they had proven themselves to be, I was going home instead of them. I felt, and still feel, that these men deserved to come home more than I did.

I stay in touch with them too, five years later. I still speak to Shane and Justin two to three times per month on the phone, and to Trueblood about once per month via the prison's secure messaging. In fact, Shane called me as I was writing this. I have told them how I felt, and they always respond by being humble, kind, and loving. They always tell me that they are so proud of me, that they belong where they are for the things that they did decades ago, and that I never belonged there with them. Such things resonated with my soul and made me feel an even deeper sadness, because they prove how much more these men deserved to be free than I did, and how much love and kindness they each had.

Two weeks before I was scheduled to come home, a young Hispanic male tried to pick a fight with me, because I stepped in front of him when he was watching TV. Three inmates stepped in between me and him: Z, a white supremacist who was an enforcer for ten years for the Unforgiven, had a swastika tattooed on his stomach, and had just found out his grandmother was a Jew; Justin Abercrombie, an ultraorthodox Jew in prison for three murders; and Trueblood.

"We will take this fade for Bork," they said. "He is going home, and we won't let anyone change this date. We have life sentences. So ask yourself: How bad do you want to die? We won't fight you. We will just kill you to make sure he goes home."

A tear developed in my eye, and I wiped it away before anyone could notice.

EPILOGUE

Somehow, I managed to make it to my release date, although I couldn't sleep during the entire week before I was supposed to be leaving. Two days before I was set to go home, I celebrated my thirtieth birthday. I sold everything that I had worth selling in order to get enough canteen food products to make a birthday goulash. I made enough to share with the people who have kept my head afloat through the darkness: Trueblood, Shane, Josh, Justin, all celebrated my birthday with me.

Using ramen noodles, buffalo pretzel pieces, relish packets, mayonnaise packets, sardines from the canteen, tomatoes smuggled from the chow hall, onions smuggled from the chow hall, Flaming

Hot Cheetos, and anything else we could put together, we created the biggest burrito you've ever seen. It was spread out on an entire bunk, four feet long and two feet deep, two inches tall. We had so much food, that I started giving it away to anybody else in the dormitory who was hungry.

When we had given away all the food we couldn't eat, Shane, Andy, Josh, and Trueblood surprised me with a birthday cake. They used oatmeal, honey buns, and cookies to create a cake, and used Kool-Aid packets to make a strawberry-frosting drizzle. I actually did cry this time, and everybody but Shane pretended not to notice. Shane put his hand on my shoulder, and with a small smile said, "I am really going to miss you too, Bork. I don't like many people, and even though you are a pain in the ass, I am gonna miss you."

On September 8, 2018, at approximately 10:00 a.m., my name was called to "roll it up" and head to Classification. I gave away anything that I had left and headed to the front of the compound. Any clothing that I had when I was arrested has long since been destroyed, and it would not have fit me anyway. I was arrested at nearly 300 pounds and I was leaving at 175 pounds. When I got up to Classification, the gate officer provided me with a donated polo shirt and a donated pair of pants, which I put on as fast as I could. I sat at the front gate waiting to leave, and I could see my family out in the parking lot. My Dad and stepmom were there, and my Mom and stepdad were present also. After what seemed like an eternity, I was allowed to leave. I got fingerprinted again and handed some paperwork, but then I was finally allowed to walk out the door as a free man. It felt so good.

I made it my mission to find a job as fast as possible. It took me three weeks to find a company willing to hire me. I found a plumbing company in Kendall, nearly one and a half hours south, willing to hire me at sixteen dollars per hour. The owner of the company was a Marine Corps veteran, and because I was a Marine Corps veteran,